Why the world still needs the F-word

About the author

Nikki van der Gaag has been an independent consultant working on gender in development, with a particular focus on girls and on men and gender equality, since 2002. She is the author of *Feminism and men* (Zed Books, 2014) and the *No-nonsense Guide to Women's Rights* (New Internationalist, 2008) and co-author of the *State of the World's Fathers* (MenCare, 2015) as well as principal author of many of Plan International's *State of the World's Girls* reports. She is a former editor at New Internationalist and is Director of Gender Justice and Women's Rights at Oxfam GB. This book was written in a personal capacity.

To Rosa and the next generations of feminists.

About the New Internationalist

New Internationalist is an award-winning, independent media co-operative. Our aim is to inform, inspire and empower people to build a fairer, more sustainable planet.

We publish a global justice magazine and a range of books, both distributed worldwide. We have a vibrant online presence and run ethical online shops for our customers and other organizations.

– **Independent media:** we're free to tell it like it is – our only obligation is to our readers and the subjects we cover.

– **Fresh perspectives:** our in-depth reporting and analysis provide keen insights, alternative perspectives and positive solutions for today's critical global justice issues.

– **Global grassroots voices:** we actively seek out and work with grassroots writers, bloggers and activists across the globe, enabling unreported (and under-reported) stories to be heard.

NONONSENSE

FEMINISM
Why the world still needs the F-word

Nikki van der Gaag

New Internationalist

NONONSENSE

Feminism
Why the world still needs the F-word

Published in 2017 by
New Internationalist Publications Ltd
The Old Music Hall
106-108 Cowley Road
Oxford OX4 1JE, UK
newint.org

Editor: Jo Lateu
Cover design: Ian Nixon
Design concept: Andrew Smith, asmithcompany.co.uk

Series editor: Chris Brazier
Series design by Juha Sorsa

Printed and bound in Great Britain by Bell & Bain Ltd, Glasgow
who hold environmental accreditation ISO 14001.

MIX
Paper from
responsible sources
FSC® C007785
FSC
www.fsc.org

British Library Cataloguing-in-Publication Data.
A catalogue record for this book is available from the British Library.

Library of Congress Cataloging-in-Publication Data.
A catalog for this book is available from the Library of Congress.

ISBN 978-1-78026-327-4
(ISBN ebook 978-1-78026-328-1)

Contents

Foreword

Growing up in Uganda in the 1960s, I was my father's daughter. I admired him very much, and people said I was like him. I had a more difficult relationship with my mother, but as I grew older and reflected on who I am and why I believe the things that I believe, I found myself coming back to my mother and my grandmother. I identified deeply with the struggles they went through, and how their struggles made them who they were – so that they could also shape me.

My mother left her teaching job to raise us and became a community leader. She built networks with women in the village, and started village women's clubs. When I was growing up, the majority of women had no formal education at all. So they learnt how to read and write through those clubs, they learnt about homemaking, childcare, sanitation and hygiene, nutrition, income generation, important life skills. The women's movement in Uganda grew from these roots.

Many years later, when I was contesting a seat in parliament, I used to recall something an uncle had said to me: 'Winnie, I have one child and three miserable girls.' In his mind, the girls were not counted as his children. Whenever I shared this on the campaign trail, the women would all start shaking their heads and I would begin to discuss gender issues with them.

Today, women are still talking about their rights, or lack of them. They are also still taking action, in myriad ways and across the globe.

Feminism was once a dirty word, rejected even by some women's rights activists; now, it is being adopted by a new generation that can see both the gains made by their elders and the threats to this progress – be it from poverty, economic inequality, religious fanaticism or climate change.

Our world seems much smaller in the 21st century,

with new media and digital innovation proving useful tools in campaigning and raising awareness. But many of the threats to women's rights remain the same as they were for my mother and grandmother: a patriarchal society that values men, and boys' education, above women and girls, in which women do menial jobs for minimum pay and face domestic violence, and in which they are silenced if they dare to speak out.

In 2015, gender equality was enshrined in the Sustainable Development Goals, as well as in the review of agreements seminal to women's rights, including the Beijing Platform for Action and UN Security Resolution 1325. There is a greater understanding that improving the state of the world's women will improve men's lives, too, and more girls across the globe are completing primary education, at least. There are more women role models – in politics, in sport, in the arts, and beyond. There is more awareness that feminism and women's rights embrace other rights and struggles, including disability, race and sexuality.

Highlighted in this informative and concise guide to feminism by Nikki van der Gaag are many individuals and groups doing incredible outreach and campaigning work, often at significant personal risk. Let us take inspiration from them – and join them in creating a fairer, more feminist 21st century.

Winnie Byanyima
Executive Director, Oxfam International

Introduction

I can't quite believe how many books on feminism I have managed to accumulate over the course of more than 20 years of working on women's rights. The piles are so high on my desk that they block the view out of my office – and they keep toppling over. Some date back to my teenage years, some were published just this month. And I wonder why I am writing another one...

But then I look at them again and I remember my younger self and how inspired I was by those who had gone before me – Alice Walker and Nawal el Saadawi and Germaine Greer and Betty Friedan and Maya Angelou and Dale Spender and Juliet Mitchell and Susan Faludi and Lynne Segal and Urvashi Butalia. I remember all the amazing women and girls in different parts of the world who shared their ideas and their stories, often harrowing ones, with me, and asked me to share them with the world.

I also remember how difficult it was to be 'out' as a feminist in the doldrums of the post-feminist 1990s, when I was juggling children and a job and my partner was the only man in his office who took a day off 'just' to be with our children.

Today, feminism is back in fashion. Rarely a day goes past when there isn't an article or a controversy, often written or fuelled by young women (and some men) who have no problem with the term – though that doesn't mean they don't still suffer for it.

Other things have not improved, and some have even got worse – violence against women, the fact that women still do the majority of poorly paid and insecure jobs as well as the unpaid work and care in the home, and the political and religious backlash in so many countries against the hard-fought rights that women have won. The fact that even the US has never had a woman president, and that misogynistic discourse is seen as acceptable even at the highest levels, means that we must all work harder than ever to ensure that women's rights are upheld, or risk worldwide rollbacks in gender equality.

The many feminisms of today are both more diverse and more argumentative, sometimes in ways that drive me mad but mostly in ways that make me proud to call myself a feminist. Sexuality, including transgender, is open and out – though not without its setbacks. There is better recognition of the things that divide women – race and ethnicity, class and caste, sexuality, disability, geography, history... though we still struggle with this every day. The internet has transformed, for better or for worse, the ways in which we can address the things we care about.

So many things are so much better for so many women. More girls are going to school than ever before. We have (some) women presidents and CEOs. Women all over the world know their rights – even if many cannot claim them. And much of that is down to feminism, whether we call it by its true name or not. Other things have not improved – violence against women, the lack of women in positions of power, the backlash of both austerity and religious extremism against women, the fact that we still do the majority of poorly paid and insecure jobs as well as the unpaid work and care in the home. The list is a long one.

This book explains the gains and the losses, the challenges and the setbacks, associated with being a feminist in the world today. It gives you some facts to fight with. It is a call for all of us – men as well as women – to join the struggle for a fairer world. Because solidarity is what feminism is all about. And it is still sorely needed: millions of women and girls all over the world continue to face violence, sexism and discrimination and are treated like second-class citizens.

Finally, it is a celebration of feminists past, present and to come. Thank you for helping to shape my life.

Nikki van der Gaag

1 Making a little trouble

'Whatever you choose, however many roads you travel, I hope that you choose not to be a lady. I hope you will find some way to break the rules and make a little trouble out there. And I also hope you will choose to make some of that trouble on behalf of women.'

Nora Ephron, US screenwriter, novelist, producer and director

Feminism has achieved a huge amount in many countries – but there is still much to be done, particularly for women and girls who face multiple disadvantages such as those caused by racism or poverty. Feminism has many faces, and there is ongoing debate about what the word even signifies. But one thing is clear: we need to put aside our differences and work together to fight for our rights.

Feminism has always been challenging, exciting and controversial. To be a feminist you need to have a keen mind, a big heart, a sense of humor – and a thick skin. You need to be prepared, in Nora Ephron's words, to 'make a little trouble'.

Although feminism has emerged from the doldrums of the 1990s and early 2000s, to call yourself a feminist today you still need to be brave. Talking to feminists in different parts of the world, I always come away with a huge sense of admiration for all that they are trying to achieve, often in the face of enormous odds – as the stories in this book reveal.

Despite this, it is heartening to see how, in the past few years, young women (and some young men) in particular have been increasingly happy to call themselves feminists and to claim spaces, online and offline, where they declare that they will no longer be second-class citizens.

French intellectual, writer and feminist Simone de

Beauvoir wrote in her book *The Second Sex* in 1949 that 'one is not born, but rather becomes, a woman'. She believed passionately that women were in no way inferior to men, despite the way that they were treated, and her call is now being taken up by the latest generation of feminists all over the world.

It is as necessary now as it was then. The United Nations estimates that it will take 80 years to achieve gender equality. That is far too long. Feminism is as relevant today as it has ever been – and as contested, as this book will show.

Calling yourself a feminist

Feminism is back in fashion. A 2016 survey in the US found that:

- 6 in 10 women and a third of men call themselves a feminist or strong feminist.
- 7 in 10 say the movement is empowering.
- Over 4 in 10 see the movement as angry, and a similar proportion say it unfairly blames men for women's challenges.
- Younger women are more optimistic about the feminist movement than older women.
- More than 4 in 10 younger women say they have expressed their views about women's rights on social media.
- The two demographic groups who identified most as feminists were 18 to 34-year-olds (63 per cent) and 50 to 64-year-olds (68 per cent).[1]

A global poll by the Pew Research Center in 2015 found that 'gender equality is among the most widely accepted democratic principles around the world'.[2] In the survey, which covered 38 countries, 65 per cent overall said they believe it is *very* important that women have the same rights as men, although in 24 of the countries, women were more likely than men to support gender equality.

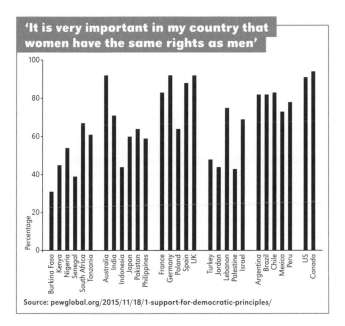

'It is very important in my country that women have the same rights as men'

Percentage (y-axis: 0, 20, 40, 60, 80, 100)

Countries (x-axis): Burkina Faso, Kenya, Nigeria, Senegal, South Africa, Tanzania, Australia, India, Indonesia, Japan, Pakistan, Philippines, France, Germany, Poland, Spain, UK, Turkey, Jordan, Lebanon, Palestine, Israel, Argentina, Brazil, Chile, Mexico, Peru, US, Canada

Source: pewglobal.org/2015/11/18/1-support-for-democratic-principles/

Not all those who work for gender equality call themselves feminists; in some contexts and societies it is too difficult, or even downright dangerous to do so, and it is therefore easier to talk about gender equality or even women's rights. 'Many women hesitate to call themselves feminists,' explains Ajete Kerqeli, a feminist and activist in Kosovo. 'It has a negative connotation here. People have said to me, "You are like the ISIS [Daesh] of gender issues!"'[3]

Sri Danti Anwar, Secretary of the Ministry for Women's Empowerment and Child Protection in Indonesia, told me: 'There is resistance to the word [feminist] because it is seen as Western. We have to relate the idea of gender equality to people's lives. That is the real challenge, not the language itself.'[4]

Even in the US, students who ran a 'Who needs feminism?' campaign acknowledged: 'Identify yourself

Making a little trouble

as a feminist today and many people will immediately assume you are a man-hating, bra-burning, whiny liberal... Feminism is both misunderstood and denigrated regularly on a broad societal scale... We encourage you all to keep defining it for yourselves!'[5]

'Feminist movements everywhere in the world are born of the particular political and economic realities of the places where they exist,' says Indian feminist publisher Urvashi Butalia. 'In that sense, each movement has different issues and concerns.' But, she believes: 'Despite cultural and economic differences, there are issues that women share worldwide that have been the concern of feminists.'[6]

And Samantha Eyler, from Colombia, expresses the opinion that 'a universal conception of feminism does exist – it's just not in the possession of one particular geographical wing of the movement. Rather, it's a truth that we international women's activists must forge together.'[7]

Feminism: definitions

It was French activist Hubertine Auclert who, in 1882, first defined the term positively as the struggle for the improvement of women's lives.[8]

Rebecca West, a writer and activist, offered another definition in 1913: 'I myself have never been able to find out precisely what feminism is,' she said. 'I only know that people call me a feminist whenever I express sentiments that differentiate me from a doormat.'

The Merriam-Webster dictionary definition of feminism is quite straightforward: 'The belief that men and women should have equal rights and opportunities'. Wikipedia says feminism is 'a range of political movements, ideologies and social movements that share a common goal: to define, establish and achieve equal political, economic, personal and social rights for women'.[9]

Long-time feminist activist, academic and writer bell hooks offers something similar, making a clear link to dismantling patriarchy: 'Simply put, feminism is a movement to end sexism, sexist exploitation, and oppression.'[10]

What has feminism achieved?

The roles that women play in the world today are in many countries almost unrecognizable from those played by their grandmothers. Women and girls in so many places are viewed in very different ways than they used to be, and participate in public life much more that they did even 50 years ago, as will become clear in later chapters, but it is worth pointing out here four important areas where they have taken place.

First, most countries have in the past few decades signed conventions and passed laws to promote equality between women and men. For example, 139 constitutions include guarantees of gender equality; 125 countries outlaw domestic violence; 117 have equal-pay laws; 173 guarantee paid maternity leave; and 29 have quotas to promote women's political participation. Women have equal rights to own property in 115 countries, and equal inheritance rights in 93. Though we will see that laws alone are not enough, they are a step in the right direction.

Second, although men still hold the majority of public positions of power, women now make up 40 per cent of the world's formal labor force. This may often be in low-paid contract work, and does not address the continuing gender pay gap, but it is still a significant shift. And there is a small but increasing minority of women who are presidents and prime ministers, CEOs and small-business owners.

Third, more girls are going to school than ever before.[11] While education is not the only solution to gender inequalities, being educated gives women more independence, including the possibility of financial independence. It also means that they are less likely to marry early and against their will, more likely to use family planning and other preventative health practices for themselves and their families, and more likely to send their children – especially their daughters – to school.[12]

Fourth, while 100 years ago women were able to vote in national elections in only four countries, today they can in every country except Saudi Arabia and the Vatican.

Most of these changes have been brought about by feminism, in the guise of organized women making exactly the kind of 'trouble' that Nora Ephron talked about. These are women who have refused to take no for an answer – and many have paid for it with their lives.

Gains under threat

So why do we still need feminism? Some people, particularly in the Global North, still claim that we do not, and that the goals of feminism have now been achieved. But we do not need to look far to see how easy they are to roll back – the misogyny revealed in the 2016 US Presidential elections showed this all too clearly.

If we look in detail at the situation in many countries, however, we can see that despite the many improvements in women's and girls' lives, and commitments to their rights, we live in times which challenge the achievement of social justice in all its forms. 'Experience shows that even women's rights victories that were won decades ago are under fresh threat of reversal – such

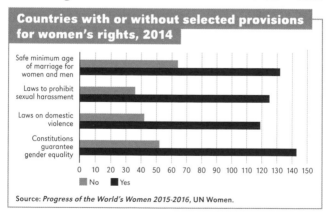

Countries with or without selected provisions for women's rights, 2014

Source: *Progress of the World's Women 2015-2016*, UN Women.

as reproductive choice, access to basic education [and] freedom of movement,' notes a report by the Association for Women's Rights in Development (AWID).[13]

Rising extremism, violent conflict, economic crises, unemployment and climate change are just a few of the major problems in the world today (see Chapter 3). Inequalities of all kinds continue to increase. The richest one per cent of the world's people own approximately 40 per cent of the world's assets, while the poorest 50 per cent own less than one per cent (see Chapter 2).[14]

The latest UN 'Progress of Women' report notes: 'Financial globalization, trade liberalization, the ongoing privatization of public services and the ever-expanding role of corporate interests in the development process have shifted power relations in ways that undermine the enjoyment of human rights and the building of sustainable livelihoods.'[15]

Austerity policies are rolling back state provision where it exists, which means that, increasingly, families and individuals are struggling. This has particular effects on women and girls, as we will see later. For example, because women are still largely responsible for unpaid work and childcare in the home, they bear the brunt of the closure of nursery provision or cutbacks in social services.[16]

An increasingly unequal world sees thousands killed in murderous wars while others live in comfort. It sees desperate people packed into small boats on the Mediterranean, fleeing conflict or poverty for safer but unwelcoming shores. It sees youth unemployment on an unprecedented scale. And it sees gender discrimination interact with geography, class, ethnicity, location, sexuality or disability in ways that mean women and girls who are already marginalized find themselves even more discriminated against.

Violence against women remains an epidemic. And it cuts across race, class and geography. Globally, one in three women still faces violence from an intimate partner.[17] Women are regularly subjected to misogyny and abuse – something which has exploded with the rise of the internet.

Or take maternal mortality. Though it dropped by 44 per cent between 1990 and 2015,[18] still 830 women die from preventable causes related to pregnancy and childbirth *every day*. All but one per cent of these deaths occur in countries of the Global South. The maternal mortality ratio ranges from 2,054 per 100,000 live births in South Sudan to 2 per 100,000 live births in Estonia.

Other comparisons are equally stark. In Latin America, indigenous women are more than twice as likely to be illiterate as non-indigenous women.[19] Gay marriage is now legal in 24 countries, but 76 countries have criminal laws against sexual activity by lesbian, gay, bisexual, transgender or intersex (LGBTI) people.[20,21]

Some of these setbacks are happening in direct response to the rights that women have won. As Sheela Patel of the Society for the Promotion of Area Resource Centers (SPARC) in India notes: 'When you work for women's interests, it's two steps forward – if you're really smart and very lucky! – and at least one step back. And those steps back are, ironically, often evidence of your effectiveness, because they represent the threat you have posed to the power structure and its attempt to push you back.'[22]

The Global Gender Gap Index was introduced by the World Economic Forum in 2006. It aimed to track the progress of gender inequality, benchmarking national gender gaps in economics, politics, education and health, and providing country rankings.[23] It shows that even in the richest countries, change does not always mean progress. The UK, for example, fell from 13th position in 2008 to 18th in 2015. In the same period, the US dropped from 27th to 28th.

Which is why a group of women students at Duke University in the US ran a campaign called 'Who needs feminism?' which went viral as people posted selfies with placards round their necks saying things like:

- 'I need feminism because "men's jobs" (like engineering and physician) pay more than "women's" jobs. And that is not okay!'
- 'I need feminism because when I was a kid my family told me that girls couldn't be pretty and smart at the same time.'
- 'I need FEMINISM because when talking about women's rights, someone came up to me and said, "Women are only good for keeping our stomachs full and our testicles empty."'[25]

Amy Annette, Martha Mosse and Alice Stride, editors of a collection of essays entitled *I Call Myself a Feminist: the view from twenty-five women under thirty*, summed it up:

'We need feminism because girls are shot in the head for going to school. We need feminism because women are burned alive for refusing to submit to gross male desire. We need feminism because women are under-represented in every sphere of life except for being wives and mothers. We need feminism because one in five women in the UK experiences sexual violence and is usually blamed and shamed for it. We need feminism because women's bodies remain politicized, scrutinized, fetishized. There are countless more reasons why we need feminism... We have allies the world over, and feminism is no longer seen only as a women's issue... We know that young feminists are out there in droves. We ARE you. This one's for you. This one's for us.'

Many feminisms, not one

The ideological richness of feminism has had a profound and radical impact on society, culture and language in many very different places. But, like any social movement, feminists are also divided by race, class, sexuality and geography, and take different positions on issues such as prostitution/sex work and pornography, democracy, militarization, peace and security, nationalism, religion, sexualities, development, globalization, privatization, private profit, private property, access and control over resources, food security, social securities, macro-economics, military expenditures, property rights, or North-South debates.

Perhaps the most contested areas have been around race, power and privilege, with some feminists from the Global South and black feminists feeling that feminism was and is driven mainly by Northern, white, middle-class women who are concerned about the glass ceiling and the gender pay gap, rather than about poverty or violence or oppression.

American feminist blogger Jessica Hoffman wrote in her 'Letter to white feminists': 'Privilege is a kind of poison – insidious, it obscures, misleads, confuses – and this is part of how power is maintained, as well-meaning privileged people miss the mark, can't clearly see what's going on and how we're implicated, are able to comfortably see ourselves as not responsible'. For Hoffman, white feminists need to see the implications of their power and privilege, or they will never be able to

The African Feminist Forum Charter

In November 2006, in Accra, Ghana, the African Feminist Forum brought together over 100 feminist activists from all over the region and the diaspora. They drew up a Charter: 'We define and name ourselves publicly as Feminists because we celebrate our feminist identities and politics. We recognize that the work of fighting for women's rights is deeply political, and the process of naming is political too. Choosing to name ourselves Feminist places us in a clear ideological position. By naming ourselves as Feminists we politicize the struggle for women's rights, we question the legitimacy of the structures that keep women subjugated, and we develop tools for transformatory analysis and action. We have multiple and varied identities as African Feminists. We are African women; we live here in Africa and even when we live elsewhere, our focus is on the lives of African women on the continent. Our Feminist identity is not qualified with 'Ifs', 'Buts', or 'Howevers'. We are Feminists. Full stop.'[26]

be part of something wider than the limits of their own lives, 'the profound, intergenerational, cross-cultural grassroots work that is transforming not only the feminist movement but all social-change movements'.[27]

Minna Salami, the Nigerian-Finnish blogger also known as Ms Afropolitan, notes:

'The idea that it is un-African to be feminist flourishes. Thankfully, a large number of women are unperturbed by such ideas. We are proud and happy to be African and feminist. Why? Because it is part of our history, to fight the power, be it male or white supremacy, and to rise. To be an African feminist today is to be part of an influential, vibrant, exciting force.'[28]

Brazilian-American blogger Juliana Britto Schwartz agrees: 'Many... argue that the term "feminist" in itself only represents privileged white women, but I've decided to stick with it... The point of this blog is to bridge movements and, by qualifying our feminism, I think we can still collaborate with allies in a way that would be harder if we were to completely separate ourselves.'[29]

Feminism like water: an intergenerational discussion[30]

What can different generations of feminists learn from one another? Leading Indian grassroots activist and author, 68-year-old Kamla Bhasin, *connects with 16-year-old Londoner* Lilinaz Evans, *co-founder of the Twitter Youth Feminist Army.*

Why do we still need feminism?

Kamla Bhasin: I believe that sexism is all pervading, it's global. And if you're born in a country that claims to have got independence, which says that men and women are equal, then at every step you find that that is not the case. For example, today, everything is gendered. Umbrellas are gendered, watches are gendered, handkerchiefs are gendered, every damn thing. And in India we have also a very gendered language. Everything small is feminine and everything large is masculine. So this whole thing is just going from bad to worse; we cannot fight gender inequality without fighting this economic system where god is profit.

Lili: I think patriarchy is a result of capitalism. That's one of the ways that feminism is misrepresented – it's never represented as the fight against capitalism and its products: it's always presented as, oh I want a job.

What kind of feminist are you?

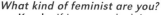

Kamla: If I were pushed, I would say I am an eco-feminist, a socialist feminist – I see the links between rape of women and rape of Mother Nature. I see links between all other forms of oppression: class, caste and race. Feminism will keep changing because patriarchy is constantly changing, constantly renewing itself, coming in newer phases. The power of patriarchy has increased so many fold. If we had to fight only our traditional patriarchies, we might have succeeded.

Lili: Second-wave feminism did a huge amount, especially around laws and equality; however, it was incredibly racist, at least in the West, transphobic and homophobic, a lot of the time. The third wave started to move towards violence against the everyday woman, but again it was still very transphobic and quite racist, especially in America. And now we're maybe on the fourth or fifth wave, we've got this globalized media which more people have access to and it brings us a more intersectional viewpoint. I hope we will soon no longer have these oppressive attitudes within feminism.

What are your priorities in terms of activism?

Lili: Focusing on a more inclusive way of getting younger women into feminism. It shouldn't be accepted that you're harassed on the street, or that you starve yourself to be thinner. But also feminism should be for all women, not just for white or fair, richer women.

Kamla: I totally echo this. I have spent my life training or talking to younger women. Patriarchy is all around us and we have to keep looking at the interconnectedness of it all. All issues are women's issues. Rape is not just a feminist issue; it's everybody's issue.

How do we achieve this?

Lili: I like that quote, 'Well-behaved women rarely make history'. We didn't get the vote by asking nicely. Feminist anger is always presented by the media as irrational and 'what are these crazy people talking about?' Anger and passion are important in de-normalizing these sexist experiences that we have, but we have to use it constructively and not just be really angry everywhere, to no purpose.

Kamla: Yes, I agree. Feminism is like water. It's everywhere but it takes the shape of the container into which it is poured. My feminism is different from Lili's feminism because I live in India, because my patriarchy is different, my technology is different. But in order to succeed, feminism has to be a global movement, because patriarchy is global, capitalism is global, racism is global: so we need to be fighting them all together, on all fronts.

Illustrations: Lulu Kitololo/Asilia

Making a little trouble

Ismahane Chouder, vice-president of the *Collectif des Féministes pour l'Egalité* (Feminist Collective for Equality), says: 'I'm a Western, Muslim feminist, and I work on campaigns across the board for all women's rights.'[31]

There are divisions too between younger and older feminists, as the dialogue between Kamla Bhasin and Lilinaz Evans shows (see pages 22-23).

FRIDA, The Young Feminist Fund,[32] supports young feminists to create exactly the kind of global movement that Kamla describes. It is the only youth-led participatory fund focused exclusively on supporting global young feminist organizing, activists and groups. 'FRIDA envisions a world where young women, girls and trans youth are recognized as experts of their own reality, can enjoy and exercise their human rights, and have the power to build a more just and sustainable world based on their own vision,' says Chloe Safier, a consultant with FRIDA. 'It currently funds over 70 groups in the Global South, using a participatory model where the power to decide where and how resources flow is in the hands of young feminists themselves.'

Other divisions within the feminist movement, which are explored in later chapters, are around sex work – is it work or exploitation? Should it be called sex work or prostitution? And, more recently, there have been heated debates around transgender, with some feminists feeling that men who have transitioned should not be viewed as women, and others taking the opposite view. Transfeminism, argues one article, represents 'a move away from viewing sexism as an overly simplistic, unilateral form of oppression, where men are the oppressors and women are the oppressed, end of story'.[33]

Finally, there are differences about whether men can be included in the feminist movement, with some arguing strongly that, as the oppressors, they can be supporters but not part of the movement, and others believing equally strongly that without the careful involvement of the growing men for gender equality movement, feminism will not succeed. In my book *Feminism and Men*, I point out:

'Gender inequality deprives women of their rights and men of their humanity. A return to traditional versions of masculinity and femininity, however much religious conservatives and men's rights movements may want it, is not an option. Women will not go back into their boxes. It is men who now need to change; to give up some of their power and privilege in the interests of freeing themselves from the historically narrow model of what it means to be male... It is time for feminism to actively include men, and for men to embrace feminism. The struggle for gender equality depends on it.'[34]

But we also need to recognize that there is a men's rights movement that is both increasingly loud, especially online, and increasingly misogynistic. We need the men who oppose this, who are for equality and against violence against women, to stand up and say so.

Our diversity is our strength

This chapter has looked at what feminism has achieved. It has examined why we still need feminism, and attempted some definitions. It has shown the many faces of feminism, and the points and issues where we agree or disagree. And it has argued that feminists need to celebrate our differences, and, in Nora Ephron's words, make a little trouble, in order to build a more equal world. As Madeleine Rees from the Women's International League for Peace and Freedom notes:

'Feminists are diverse; different races and backgrounds, all colors, shapes and sizes, but our diversity is our strength. It's what makes us a brilliant though flawed species, and, if we could embrace that thought, it's what could build a serious and effective movement for change.'[35]

1 *The Washington Post* and Kaiser Family Foundation, 2016. nin.tl/USfeminism **2** Pew Research Center, 2015. nin.tl/pew-support **3** Personal conversation with the author. **4** Nikki van der Gaag, *Feminism and Men*, Zed Books, London, 2014. **5** whoneedsfeminism.tumblr.com **6** *Granta*, nin.tl/granta-urvashi **7** nin.tl/eyler-exporting-feminism **8** Isabelle Ernot, 'Sociétés industri-elles: un siècle de mutations', in Geneviève Dermenjian, Irène Jami, Annie Rouquier et al, *La place des femmes dans l'histoire: une histoire mixte*, Éditions Belin, Paris, 2011. **9** en.wikipedia.org/wiki/Feminism **10** nin.tl/bellhookspain **11** ungei.org **12** UNICEF, nin.tl/unicef-girls **13** Srilatha Batliwala, *Women Moving Mountains: Collective Impact of the Dutch MDG3*, Association of Women's Rights in Development, 2013. **14** UNDP, *Humanity Divided: Confronting Inequality in Developing Countries*, New York, 2013. **15** UN Women, *Progress of the World's Women 2015-2016: Transforming Economies, Realizing Rights*, New York, 2015. **16** UN Women, *The Global Economic Crisis and Gender Equality*, NewYork, 2014. **17** UN Women, *Progress of the World's Women*, op cit. **18** WHO, nin.tl/who-mm **19** UN Women, *Progress of the World's Women*, op cit. **20** nin.tl/76-crimes **21** nin.tl/forbes-gaymarriage **22** Srilatha Batliwala and Alexandra Pittman, *Capturing Change in Women's Realities: A Critical Overview of Current Monitoring & Evaluation Frameworks and Approaches*, Association of Women's Rights in Development, 2010. **23** nin.tl/GGGreport2015 **24** nin.tl/GGGR2015 **25** whoneedsfeminism.tumblr.com **26** African Feminist Forum, nin.tl/aff-preamble **27** Alternet, nin.tl/alternet-open-letter **28** *The Guardian*, nin.tl/vibrant-africa **29** Foreign Affairs, nin.tl/fa-eyler **30** nin.tl/women-edge **31** *The Guardian*, nin.tl/islamic-feminists **32** youngfeministfund.org **33** Ms., nin.tl/Ms-transfeminism **34** Nikki van der Gaag, op cit. **35** Open Democracy, nin.tl/gender-war-peace

The struggle for equality and the emancipation of women has not always been called feminism. But the roots of feminist thinking and action go back long before the suffragettes and are no means confined to the Global North...

1 Rebels and thinkers

In sixth-century BCE Greece, Sappho wrote lesbian poetry and ran a girls' school. The 15th-century French writer Christine de Pisan is now regarded as a feminist thinker. In the 17th century English adventurer and political activist Aphra Behn was getting embroiled in the West Indian slave rebellion – and writing 19 plays and four novels.

2 Mothers of the revolution

Women played a major role in the 1789 French Revolution and the ideal of 'Republican Motherhood' took shape. But, some argued, if women had the task of 'bringing up the new citizens', they should also have status. Feminist pamphlets proliferated. In her *Rights of Woman*, Olympe de Gouges wrote: 'Woman is born free and her rights are the same as those of man... if women have the right to go to the scaffold, they must also have the right to go to Parliament.' Parisian women formed political clubs and associations to campaign on issues affecting them. But the male leaders of the Revolution were basically hostile and in 1793 they outlawed all women's clubs. A woman's place was in the home, they ruled. This hostility persisted through the 19th century. The Napoleonic Code gave all management of family funds to the husband. Not until 1909 did French women have control over their own earnings. Not until 1944 did they get the vote.

3 Radical sparks

Meanwhile, in North America, women took part in the inde-pendence struggle and exercised their power as consumers to boycott British goods. Even in Britain there was a rash of radical – and reactionary – writing about women. Closely watching events in France was British journalist and translator Mary Wollstonecraft. She worked to support her family but in 1787 came to London to live by her writing. She joined a radical circle of intellectuals. A year after Thomas Paine wrote *The Rights of Man* (1791) Mary Wollstonecraft produced *A Vindication of the Rights of Woman*. It was the first full-scale book favoring women's liberation and was widely read. She was dismissed by the male conservative press as 'a strumpet'.

4 Missions and manacles

For black women living in slavery in the US, the late 18th century was a turning point, as Protestant evangelism combined with the anti-slavery movement. Women made up a large part of revival congregations – both in white and black churches. Women were not supposed to preach, but some – like former slave Jarena Lee – ignored this. Black women realized that freedom from whites was not enough. They had to have freedom from men too. But uniting white and black women was not easy. When black feminist Sojourner Truth stood before the Second Annual Convention of Women's Rights in Akron Ohio in 1852, white racist women tried to stop her speaking. There were many black women activists but Sojourner Truth was the most outspoken, arguing publicly that black women should have the vote.

5 Industry and protest

During the Industrial Revolution, unmarried women were leaving home to work in the cities, often for low wages in appalling factory conditions. Meanwhile, the idea of female education became firmly entrenched and middle-class women were demanding access to a much wider range of occupations. On both sides of the Atlantic women started taking part in industrial action. During the 1808 weavers' strike in Britain *The Times* singled out striking women weavers as 'more turbulent and insolent' than the men. In the US the first all-women strike took place in 1828 at Cocheco Mill, New Hampshire. In Britain in 1854 Barbara Leigh Smith drew together for the first time a group of women who called themselves feminists and campaigned to change laws. A strike by women in an East London match factory helped create the British trade-union movement.

6 Invasion and rebellion

In Asia and Africa women were resisting both traditional and colonial oppression. Chinese feminists who joined the Taiping Rebellion of 1850-64 called for an end to foot-binding and demanded communal ownership of property and equal rights for women and men. In Japan in the early 20th century, feminist Kato Shidzue campaigned for birth control and other reforms. In India in 1905, women were participating in the Swadeshi movement to boycott foreign goods and in 1917 the Women's Indian Association was set up with links to the British movement for women's suffrage. In parts of Africa women were banned from entering the cities and their traditional access to land – as Africa's principal farmers – was also denied. Adelaide Casely-Hayford was a Sierra Leonean women's rights activist in the early part of the 20th century who had a pan-African vision, while in 1918 in South

Africa, Charlotte Maxeke founded the Bantu Women's League. Huda Shaarawi established the Egyptian Feminist Union, which in 1924 managed to get the age of marriage for girls raised to 16.

7 Suffering for suffrage

Women's call for the vote was echoing around the world. It was first answered in New Zealand/Aotearoa in 1893. In Britain, mass meetings organized by Emmeline Pankhurst and her two daughters Sylvia and Christabel drew crowds of up to 500,000. Determined militants chained themselves to railings and caused civil disturbances. In 1908 the Pankhursts were arrested and imprisoned. They went on hunger strike and were force-fed – causing public outcry. But only in 1918 did women (over the age of 30) get the vote in Britain. The US followed in 1920. In India, provincial assemblies were allowed to enfranchise women in 1919. And in 1931 the Indian National Congress Party pledged itself to sexual as well as caste and religious equality at independence. The first Latin American country to give women the vote was Ecuador in 1929, followed by Brazil, Argentina, Cuba and Chile during the 1930s.

8 Reds and beds

Karl Marx and Friedrich Engels saw women's liberation as part of the socialist revolution and Rosa Luxemburg, Clara Zetkin and Alexandra Kollantai became respected political leaders. In 1918 the first Women's Conference was held in Moscow and during the 1920s – under Lenin – the Soviet government promoted equal rights. Marriage, divorce and contraception were made simple. But in the 1930s and 1940s Stalin turned the clock back. Divorce was made difficult, abortion banned, contraception restricted. In China, the 1949 Revolution brought formal equality for women and men. But both here and in the USSR women did the housework as well as their jobs. In the West, feminism lay dormant. Radicals were preoccupied with fighting unemployment and fascism, and then McCarthyism. Leftwing politics was not always allied with feminist principles.

9 The Second Wave

During the 1960s, feminism burst into life again in the US as part of a radical culture that included civil rights and sexual liberation. Betty Friedan's *The Feminine Mystique* was a bestseller in 1963. Feminist groups campaigned on issues such as childcare, health, welfare, education and abortion. Consciousness-raising groups proliferated. In Europe, Canada and Australasia too, new ideas and laws were changing society. Germaine Greer's *The Female Eunuch* was an eye-opener. And in 1975 the United

Nations announced an International Decade for Women. Revolutionary movements in Zimbabwe, Angola, Mozambique and Nicaragua were including women's liberation in their ideology. In Europe the peace movement became the focus for feminist activism – especially at the US air base at Greenham Common in England. And feminism boomed in Latin America after the restoration of democracy during the 1980s.

10 Compulsory heterosexuality

The Second Wave was not without its own problems. Attitudes towards homosexuality were bitterly contested – Betty Friedan famously referred to lesbians as 'the lavender menace'. Lesbian feminism emerged out of what Adrienne Rich referred to as 'compulsory heterosexuality', and led to separatism and political lesbianism. It also hugely influenced the gay liberation movement and gave birth to Queer Theory, explored by feminist theorists such as Judith Butler, who challenged conventional notions of gender and developed a theory of gender performativity. Today, the debates around sexuality highlight transgender issues as an area of disagreement for feminists.

11 Post-feminism and the Third Wave

In the 1990s and 2000s many people talked of a 'post-feminist' age because they felt that in the Global North at least, equality had been achieved. It was a difficult time to be a feminist. So-called Third-Wave feminism rejected some of the tropes of the Second Wave, embracing high heels and make-up that the Second Wave had rejected and claiming that it was possible to be beautiful and have a brain. 'Girl Power' was born, subverting language such as Slut and Bitch.

12 Forging a new wave

Hard on the high heels of the Third Wave, Fourth-Wave feminism is in the process of emerging, with a vibrant presence on the internet. Formed within a neoliberal agenda, there is often a stress on individual freedoms, and on gender as a non-binary concept, at the same time recognizing more fully than previous incarnations how feminism is not a standalone issue, but that women are also oppressed by class, race, ability, age and sexual orientation. While the issue of men's involvement continues to create divisions, movements of men against violence against women and for new ways of being a man are increasingly part of the debates. Feminisms may change and adapt and grow, but there is no doubt that today they are alive and kicking all over the world – and still very much needed.

With thanks to Vanessa Baird, this section is expanded and adapted from her issue of New Internationalist on Feminism in 1992.

2 Feminism: a response to an unequal world

Women face multiple discriminations – not just as females, but because of their class, the color of their skin, their sexual orientation or a disability. Rising inequality has increased the risk of violence and poverty that millions of women are subjected to around the world.

Introduction: rising inequalities

We live in an increasingly unequal world. The gap between rich and poor in particular is growing wider, particularly for those who come from a minority ethnic or indigenous group, or from a lower caste or class, or who have a disability, or are not hetero-sexual. If you are also a woman or a girl, then you have an even greater chance of facing social exclusion, poverty or violence.

Growing economic inequality is bad for us all – it undermines the gains that have been made elsewhere and compounds existing inequalities. According to the International Monetary Fund (IMF), countries with higher income inequality are also likely to have greater gaps between women and men in relation to health, education, labor-market participation and political representation.[1]

More unequal societies also tend to have a higher gender pay gap. In the US, for example, young women in working-class communities face a bigger pay gap than their more middle-class peers.[2] Women constitute most of the world's low-paid workers, often in insecure, zero-hours, part-time or contract jobs or in the informal sector. Wages for this kind of work have barely increased at all; in fact, in some sectors, often those with the most women, they have decreased – in the garment

A growing gap

- In 2015, just 62 individuals (53 of whom were men) had the same wealth as the poorest 3.6 billion people in the world (or half the global population).
- The wealth of the poorest half fell by just over $1 trillion in the same period – a drop of 41 per cent.
- Since the turn of the century, the poorest half of the world's population has received just one per cent of the total increase in global wealth, while half of that increase has gone to the richest one per cent.
- The average annual income of the poorest 10 per cent has risen by less than $3 each year in almost a quarter of a century. Their daily income has risen by less than a single cent every year.

Share of Global Wealth, 2010-15

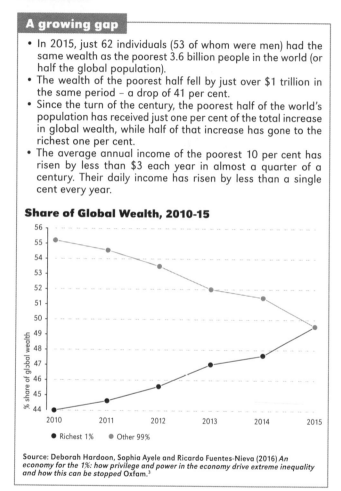

● Richest 1%   ● Other 99%

Source: Deborah Hardoon, Sophia Ayele and Ricardo Fuentes-Nieva (2016) *An economy for the 1%: how privilege and power in the economy drive extreme inequality and how this can be stopped* Oxfam.[3]

industry, for example, between 2001 and 2011, wages in most of the world's 15 main exporting countries fell in real terms.[4] At the same time, the highest salaries have increased exponentially, with CEOs in top US firms (few of them women) increasing their salaries by 54.3 per cent since 2009. An Oxfam report notes that 'the

CEO of India's top information technology firm makes 416 times the salary of a typical employee'.[5]

Another important factor in exacerbating existing inequalities between women and men in many countries is that, despite often being responsible for food production, women rarely own the land they work on, or have any security or control regarding their use of it.[6]

Bridging the gender gap: girls' education

Beyond the many structural and attitudinal changes that are needed, one way – though not the only way – of improving inequalities (between women and men but also among women themselves) is to ensure that more girls go to school. This has been a major sea change in the past 15 years, with a record number of girls now getting an education.[7]

As Aris, aged 17, from Indonesia, says: 'In the past, the difference between access to education for girls and boys was very wide. In the past 10 years this is beginning to change. Parents begin to see that it is important for both boys and girls to go to school.'[8]

Girls' education has huge benefits not only for the girls themselves, but also for their families and the wider economy. But it is still the most marginalized girls, from poor or ethnic-minority families or rural areas, who are the least likely to go to school.

But there is also a danger that by just focusing on girls' education, we ignore the growing problem in many countries of boys dropping out of school.[9] Research is clear that boys' education is good for gender equality. For example, one study in six countries found that younger men, and those with more education, had more gender-equitable views than their parents.[10] Boys who leave school early are often from poor or marginalized families; as ever, class and race play a major role. Barry Chevannes, Professor of Social Anthropology at the University of the West Indies, has no doubt that 'male

The benefits of girls' education

Early marriage
- Across 18 of the 20 countries with the highest prevalence of early marriage, girls with no education are up to six times more likely to marry as children than girls with a secondary education.[11]
- In Ethiopia in 2011, almost one in three young women with no education was married by the age of 15. Among those with a secondary education, the share was just nine per cent.[12]

Family planning
- In Punjab, Pakistan, women 'with middle- and high-school education have around 1.8 fewer children by the end of their reproductive life than those with lower than middle-school education.[13]
- In Nigeria, women with no education gave birth for the first time at age 18, on average, compared with age 25 for those with at least secondary education.[14]

Health
- In the Democratic Republic of Congo, a study interviewing 351 pregnant women found that they were three times as likely to report sleeping under a mosquito net if they had completed secondary school or higher.[15]

Earning power
- In Pakistan, working women with a high level of literacy skills earned 95 per cent more than women with weak or no literacy skills, whereas the differential was only 33 per cent among men.[16]

Access to credit
- In Kenya, education is a significant determinant of female farmers' access to formal credit, though it was not a significant determinant for male farmers.[17]

Growth and nutrition
- In Ethiopia, one-year-olds whose mothers had a primary-school education, along with access to antenatal care, were 39 per cent less likely to have stunted growth.[18]

Children's education
- In Pakistan, children whose mothers have even a single year of education spend one extra hour studying at home every day and report higher test scores.[19]

alienation from the school system contributes to all the social problems that we have come across'. He notes that boys' education can help to reduce violence and irresponsible sexual behavior, as well as other risky behaviors that affect women and girls as well as men and boys.[20]

Andreas, a young man in Indonesia, says that because of education and changes in the law, 'women are now more willing to express their opinions and men are starting to hear them. Young educated men see that the women's movement should be supported. This is a change between generations. My father would raise his eyebrows and say, "What is feminism anyway?", but, in cities at least, younger men will support women.'[21]

The gender technology divide

The other divide between women and men is technological. In terms of internet use, women lag behind men in every part of the world except the Americas. With so many jobs now dependent on access to the internet and information communication technologies (ICTs), this represents considerable lost economic, social and

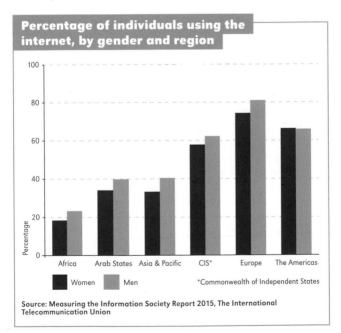

Percentage of individuals using the internet, by gender and region

Source: Measuring the Information Society Report 2015, The International Telecommunication Union

educational opportunities.

The Partnership on Measuring ICT for Development noted in 2014: 'Socio-cultural factors that cause a higher concentration of women in the uneducated, unemployed and poor segments of society also marginalize them in terms of access and use of ICTs.'[22]

Similar patterns exist in terms of global mobile-phone use. Worldwide, 1.7 billion girls and women do not own a mobile phone.[23]

- In South Asia, women are 38 per cent less likely to own a mobile phone than men.
- In Niger, they are 45 per cent less likely to own one.
- In Mexico's urban areas, women are only 2 per cent less likely to own a mobile phone, but in rural areas this rises to 26 per cent.[24]

Research in 11 countries by the GSMA Connected Women program[25] found that the top five barriers to mobile-phone ownership and use by women are:
- High cost of mobile handsets and credit
- Poor network quality and coverage
- Security concerns and harassment over mobile phones
- Lack of trust in agents and operators
- Low technical literacy and confidence.

One report estimates that closing the gender gap in mobile-phone ownership and usage could unlock an estimated $170-billion market opportunity for the mobile industry between 2015 and 2020.[26]

Black lives matter

If you are black or from a minority or indigenous group, and a woman, then you are more likely to be poor and to face discrimination and violence, wherever you live in the world. The murder of young black men in the US and the rise of the Black Lives Matter[27] movement have drawn the world's attention to such injustices.

'We need a computer more than hot food!' Girls and technology in Egypt[28]

'We badly needed a new oven, but when I talked to my children, they said that we could manage, and that we needed a computer more than hot food!' smiles Mrs Faysa wryly.

Aliya, her daughter, says that her brother is better on the computer than she is, but that she is learning fast. Even in poor areas of Alexandria like this one, young women recognize the importance of information and communications technologies. They usually have mobile phones and can find access to computers, perhaps in the house of a friend or a relative. Although a woman is 26 per cent less likely to own a phone than a man in Egypt, this gap seems to be closing for the younger generation.

Rana says she has used the internet to share experiences and even to create a magazine with other young people in her home town of Alexandria and also worldwide. Many young people say they have a Facebook and email account. Rana's friend Noura, aged 15, won a computer in a school competition and says: 'Most of our friends have computers and mobiles.'

These are girls whose parents came from the village to the town in search of a better life and whose mothers were illiterate. Now their mothers, encouraged by their daughters, are learning to read and write and recognizing the power of education and the importance of technology. Noura's mother Leila, who has two other girls, says: 'I am joining literacy classes so that I can read and write like my daughters. I never went to school, so I hope that my daughters will have a high level of education. Education is important for girls so that they can understand the world. My daughters will be better than me because I was not educated, and I suffer from not being able to read and write.'

She is delighted that Noura now has a computer in the house and immensely proud of her daughter for winning a prize. This would not have been possible back in the village, as another mother points out: 'In the village I couldn't even work. Women in rural areas still suffer a lot from discrimination, though this is beginning to change. There is more freedom for girls and women in the city now because of technology and more awareness.'

For girls like Noura, technology remains a route to discovering new ways of looking at the world. 'I couldn't live without my mobile or my computer now,' she says.

Black women, in the US and elsewhere, continue to face discrimination because they are black and because they are women:[29]

- Of the 98 women in Congress, only 14 are African American.
- Only 21.4 per cent of African American women had a college degree or higher in 2010, compared to 30 per cent of white women.
- Only 2 per cent of African American women are represented in science, technology, engineering and mathematics (STEM) fields, while women in total make up 24 per cent of the STEM workforce.
- African American women only made 64 cents to the dollar compared to white, non-Hispanic men in 2010. White women made 78.1 cents to the same dollar.

Caste – India's curse[30]

In October 2015, India awoke to a horror story. Just outside Delhi, two Dalit children, aged nine months and two-and-a-half years, were burnt to death in a ghastly tale of revenge and caste hatred.

To settle scores from an older feud, some men from a dominant caste crept up to the house of the sleeping Dalit family and poured petrol from an open window onto their bed. They set it alight and bolted the family in from outside. The children died before they arrived at a Delhi hospital. Their mother, Rekha, suffered serious burns. Their father, Jitender, also received burn injuries while trying to save his family.

Yet the children's deaths did not stop traffic in Delhi, nor seriously hit Indian TV channels. These are routine deaths. Dalit deaths. Expendable people. Caste tension is the reason attributed to their murders. Flip the page; it's not really newsworthy. Just some dead Dalits. Been going on for thousands of years. No-one is shocked. No-one gives it a second thought.

When will Dalit deaths cease to be ignored in our country? Unless casteism is eliminated from our villages, we will always remain a backward, primitive, despicable society. We rape Dalit women to teach their menfolk a lesson and keep them in their place. We kill Dalit men because they are getting too big for their boots. We prevent Dalits from studying or following their aspirations because they must stay in our villages to work, exploited and underpaid, so we can prosper.

- African American women had an unemployment rate of 10.5 per cent compared to 5.8 per cent for white women.
- The poverty rate for African American women is 28.6 per cent. In comparison, the poverty rate of white, non-Hispanic women is 10.8 per cent. The poverty rate of African American lesbian couples is 21.1 per cent versus 4.3 per cent for white lesbian couples.
- Black women are four times more likely to die from pregnancy-related causes, such as embolism and pregnancy-related hypertension, than any other racial group.
- African American women are three times more likely than white women to be incarcerated.

I have visited Dalit villages in every corner of my country. I have witnessed their pain at close quarters. I've heard Dalits scream, 'Enough. When will it end?'

We have to acknowledge the evil in our past and atone for it. We cannot provide justice to all those who died aeons ago, but we have to punish the guilty today. The rapists and murderers of Dalit women, men and children have been given impunity for centuries. They deem it their birthright.

Our Constitution, brilliantly framed by a Dalit, is moving in its rhetoric and passion about justice for all. Yet caste is the antithesis of all democratic values and belief, by its very nature. It proclaims that some people are born to be slaves to others. For millennia, dominant castes considered it their prerogative to persecute and enslave those decreed their inferiors. An enormous percentage of our population still believes this is their birthright. And they will kill to enforce these beliefs, to show their power over what they believe are 'lesser' humans.

Although we have powerful laws to enforce justice for the vulnerable, they are rarely used. Unless this changes, our society will continue to remain feudal, nasty and brutish. We can preen ourselves on the wonders of ancient India. But any thinking Indian knows that, in reality, with things the way are at present we can only hang our heads in shame.

Mari Marcel Thekaekara

If this is the case in one of the most powerful countries in the world, it is often worse in countries of the Global South. The International Work Group for Indigenous Affairs (IWGIA) notes that 'indigenous women often face double discrimination: they are discriminated as indigenous and as women. Discrimination as women they experience not only from the surrounding society but often also from within their own communities.'[31]

In India, for example, the caste system means that Dalit women, previously known as 'Untouchables', are considered the lowest of the low, whose lives are expendable. On top of this, many are still manual scavengers, who carry human excrement in dripping baskets on their heads (see box pages 38-39).

Organizing against oppression

So where do these multiple discriminations leave feminism – or, rather, feminisms?

First, these brief stories and statistics would seem to indicate that Dalit, indigenous and other minority ethnic women have only been victims. This is definitely not the case. Many have a long history of organizing against oppression. Indigenous women, for example, have long been the protectors of the earth's precious resources, and have often risked their lives in doing so.[32]

Berta Cáceres, a Honduran indigenous and environmental rights campaigner, was murdered in March 2016 for her opposition to a hydroelectric project. 'I have no doubt,' her 84-year-old mother said, 'that she has been killed because of her struggle, and that soldiers and people from the dam are responsible. I hold the government responsible.'

Interviewed by *The Guardian* a year earlier, when she won the prestigious Goldman Environmental Prize, Berta said she knew of the risks she was facing but that they did not deter her: 'We must undertake the struggle in all parts of the world, wherever we may be, because we have no other spare or replacement planet.

We have only this one, and we have to take action.'[33]

Second, black and minority ethnic women have challenged the way that feminism has sometimes been seen as singular and, as such, as white and middle-class. Black British feminist Lola Okolosie has written movingly of her mother's double oppression – by the state and wider society, and by her own husband. This meant that calling the police when he was violent was simply not an option. 'I call myself a black feminist,' Lola says, 'because I am unwilling to be silent and complicit... Emotionally, black feminism reminds black women that the racism and sexism they experience on a daily basis are not a figment of their individual imaginations but are real and structural. Critically, black feminism is championing a more nuanced understanding of how oppression and privilege operate. We, all of us, must understand that, at the level of the individual, we can at differing points occupy positions of privilege... For the feminist movement, it is also best to not repeat the mistakes of the past. It would demonstrate an inexcusable carelessness for the lives of women like my mother who are too often silenced and unheard.'[34]

Disability rights and feminism

Around 15 per cent of the global population, or roughly a billion people, live with a disability.[35] Eighty per cent of these live in developing countries,[36] perhaps because people living in poverty are more at risk of disability due to lack of proper food, healthcare and sanitation, as well as safe living and working conditions. And if they are disabled, they are even less likely to be able to access schools, employment and other services.

In many countries, women have higher rates of disability than men.[37] 'The most pressing issues faced by disabled women are the ones faced by most women, except that when you're disabled, it adds another layer of discrimination,' says Eleanor Lisney, co-founder of a disabled women's network in Britain called Sisters of Frida.[38,39]

Although accurate statistics are difficult to find, those that exist bear out her statement:[40]

- Mortality rates among girls with disabilities are much higher than for boys.
- 90 per cent of children with disabilities in developing countries do not attend school.
- Literacy rates for women with disabilities globally may be as low as one per cent.
- Only 25 per cent of women with disabilities are in the global workforce.
- Because of increased risk of gender-based violence and lack of access to reproductive health services, women with disabilities face unique challenges in preventing HIV infection.
- Women and girls with disabilities are particularly vulnerable to violence and abuse. In the US, violence against people with disabilities has been reported to be 4-10 times greater than that against people without disabilities.[41] A survey in Orissa, India, found that virtually all of the women and girls with disabilities were beaten at home, 25 per cent of women with intellectual disabilities had been raped and six per cent of women with disabilities had been forcibly sterilized.[42]

All the more reason, then, that the feminist movement needs to include women with disabilities. As British journalist Fran Ryan explained in an article in the *New Statesman* (see box, right), women with disabilities have much to offer in their understanding of the multiple oppressions that women and girls face, and in their ideas about the solutions.

Feminisms and the tyranny of the binary
One of the litmus tests of a progressive society is its treatment not only of feminists and black and minority ethnic groups, but its attitudes towards LGBTQI

'It's not only steps that keep us out': mainstream feminism must stop ignoring disabled women[43]

I was a disabled feminist around a decade after I knew I was disabled and a feminist. In retrospect, I can only think I wasn't paying attention. Or perhaps I was and that was the problem. The girls around me were not disabled. At school, or the rooms and streets at the start of adult life. I could, with no obvious contradiction, be different on a daily basis and have very little awareness of difference. When the crowd is big enough, it is easy to get lost in it. I thought about that a few years later, as feminism made its resurgence in the mainstream agenda, but did so seemingly without the faces and lives of disabled women. I thought about it again as disability rights campaigns began to get attention, but framed as separate and foreign to what matters for women. Could I be disabled on a Monday and a woman on a Tuesday? Slicing an identity has the result of a half-life – and perhaps, crucially, the movements that attempt to improve those lives failing to acknowledge the particular way being unequal in one affects being unequal in another.

This falls both ways. Issues labelled as 'disability' – for example, cuts to carers' allowance – end up rarely being seen as feminist, and feminist campaigns – such as domestic violence – existing without mention of disabled women...

Feminist and disability rights are born from a similar cloth. They are battles to acknowledge that oppression doesn't come from a biological reality but a socially constructed inequality. They are concerned with idealized human bodies. They fight the structures and power that wish to control them: in sex, in work, in reproduction.

For disabled women, sexism and disability meet to mark lives in particular ways. Increased threat of sexual and intimate partner violence. Our forced sterilization. A workplace that physically excludes us. The denial of our right to sexual support and education. The shaming of our bodies.

Disabled women's experiences reflect the bigger picture of what it is to be a woman in this society – and, in their own right, tell us about other women who also matter. There should not need to be a disabled girl in the room to know they are out there. Different women, merging into the sameness of the dominant crowd. Feminism, in all its parts, will only be richer for noticing them; listening to voices silenced by others and welcoming bodies often excluded.

Fran Ryan

(Lesbian, Gay, Bisexual, Transgender, Queer and Intersex) people.

In many countries, there has been major progress in the last decade. In 2001, the Netherlands was the first to make gay marriage legal; it has now been followed by 23 other countries. In India, as well as other countries, there is now an official box alongside 'male' and 'female' – although it means ticking yourself as 'other'.

LGBTQI people have been a major factor in the push for such change. They have always been at the forefront of challenging traditional notions of gender, and have often paid a heavy price. As with feminism, the gains made by LGBTQI communities have often led to a backlash, and LGBTQI individuals are still murdered, raped, imprisoned and even executed just for being who they are. Being homosexual is still illegal in 76 countries,[44] and in 10 the death penalty remains on the statute books.

In mid-2013 in Russia, a so-called 'gay propaganda' law was passed which criminalizes any public advocacy or campaigning for LGBTI rights.[45] In Nigeria, a law was passed in 2014 that criminalizes same-sex relationships, with penalties of up to 14 years in prison, and membership of gay organizations, for which the maximum sentence is 10 years.[46] If people do not 'turn in' gay people within 24 hours, they also face prison.[47]

In Europe, a 2013 poll found that 26 per cent of gay people and 35 per cent of transgender people said they had been attacked or threatened with violence during the past five years; 47 per cent said they had been discriminated against.[48] In South Africa, lesbians have been subject to what has come to be known as 'corrective rape'.[49]

Perhaps the most contested issue in this area for feminists has been around the growing movement for transgender rights. Since April 2015 in particular, when former Olympic athlete Caitlin Jenner transitioned to being a woman and made the cover of *Time*

Countries where homosexuality is still illegal

Source: 76crimes.com/76-countries-where-homosexuality-is-illegal/

magazine,[50] there has been a huge rise in media interest in transgender and non-binary people. In December of the same year, Tamara Adrian become the first trans candidate in Venezuela's Congress.[51]

But trans people also face high levels of violence, discrimination and abuse, resulting in major mental-health issues – suicide rates are 50 times higher than average.[52] Between 2008 and 2015, the Trans Murder Monitoring project noted 2,016 killings of trans and gender-diverse people in 65 countries.[53]

Transgender people don't only face opposition from those who want to keep men and women within strict gender norms. There was a major row in the US in July 2016 when President Obama's administration required government schools to allow transgender students to use bathrooms and locker rooms 'consistent with their gender identity'. By September of that year, 10 states had lodged a legal challenge to the policy.[54]

Many radical feminists, while acknowledging that members of the transgender community face real oppression, believe that transitioning is not a feminist strategy. Germaine Greer drew opprobrium from many other feminists by condemning Caitlin

Jenner's transition, in her usual forthright style: 'I think misogyny plays a really big part in all of this; that a man who goes to these lengths to become a woman will be a better woman than someone who is just born a woman... Just because you lop off your dick and then wear a dress doesn't make you a fucking woman.'[55]

Other feminists have challenged this view, asserting in a statement that trans people are 'essential to feminism's mission to advocate for women and other people oppressed, exploited, and otherwise margin-alized by patriarchal and misogynistic systems and people'.[56]

Supporters of transgender people within feminism have coined the term 'trans feminism'. As one *Ms.* magazine blogger put it: 'Trans feminism... is simply one of numerous third-wave feminisms that take an intersectional approach to challenging sexism and oppression. The only thing different about trans feminism is that it extends this feminist analysis to transgender issues, which have been largely overlooked or misinterpreted by feminists in the past... When trans feminism is reduced to a debate about whether trans women "count" as women or as feminists, it's a disservice not only to us but to feminism as a whole.'[57]

Writer Vanessa Baird makes very clear the link between the treatment of transgender and other non-binary people and the oppression faced by feminists: 'Trans and gender-variant people present a challenge and an opportunity for deepening equality and enlarging citizenship rights for us all. Often they strike at the root of a concept that sustains a much wider oppression: the tyranny of the binary. This tyranny serves many purposes – above all the maintenance of patriarchy. Male domination depends upon a constantly reinforced belief in the innate difference between women and men – and therefore their rights, roles and privileges. To the patriarchal mind-set, the notion that gender might be more fluid,

The challenges of being intersex

Dawn Vago has grown up with the consequences of having surgery to 'correct' an intersex variation as a child. Now 35, she is genetically male but has always looked entirely female. She has complete androgen insensitivity syndrome (CAIS): her body has XY chromosomes but is unable to respond to male sex hormones, so she developed female genitalia. Internally, she was born with testes instead of ovaries, and no uterus.

Warm and self-assured, Vago lives in Cheshire when she's not working as an entertainer on a cruise ship. She is one of only a few British intersex people prepared to speak publicly on the issue. 'My parents were told not to tell me, that I wouldn't understand and I wouldn't fit into society if I knew the shameful secret about myself,' she says. 'They wanted me to live an open and honest life, so they told me when I was five years old.' Dawn's parents were told by doctors that she would get cancer if her testes weren't removed, so she had a full gonadectomy aged eight. 'They said I would not survive puberty if I did not have the operation, and that wasn't true.'

Vago is living proof that intersex people can live successful lives while being open about being born outside traditional male and female categories. 'Doctors told my parents that I would never find a man who would love me, and I would never have my own family,' she says, a few days after her bid to adopt a child was approved. 'I absolutely adore the fact that I am married and about to start a family. It proves you control your own life.'

Dawn is now co-director of IntersexUK,[58] a campaign group founded in 2011 to end stigma around intersex variations, and to fight for equality and protection of intersex people.[59]

might not be a fact of nature but socially constructed, is as undesirable as it is inconceivable.'[60]

Conclusion: dismantling patriarchy

This chapter has shown how inequalities between women and men are intimately intertwined with inequalities due to our class, the color of our skin, our sexual orientation or whether we are disabled or not disabled. It has shown how girls' education can help to bridge these gaps – but that this must be done with care, so as not to push boys into increasingly negative behaviors. It has looked at the digital divide and how this affects women and girls.

Ultimately, the challenge that feminism throws out is to question the patriarchal structures that underpin all inequalities. In doing so, it builds a world that grows more equal, where justice is available to everyone, regardless of background, class or gender. As bell hooks, long-time feminist activist, academic and writer, said: 'Anyone who advocates feminist politics needs to understand that challenging and dismantling patriarchy is at the core of contemporary feminist struggle – this is essential and necessary if women and men are to be truly liberated from outmoded sexist thinking and actions.'[61]

1 Christian Gonzales et al, *IMF staff discussion note: Catalyst for Change: Empowering Women and Tackling Income Inequality*, IMF, 2015. **2** Bloomberg, nin.tl/widest-pay-gap **3** Oxfam, nin.tl/privilege-and-power **4** Deborah Hardoon, Sophia Ayele and Ricardo Fuentes-Nieva, *An economy for the 1%: how privilege and power in the economy drive extreme inequality and how this can be stopped* Oxfam, 2016, nin.tl/privilege-and-power **5** Oxfam, nin.tl/privilege-and-power **6** Nancy Kachingwe, *Securing women's right to land and livelihoods: a key to ending hunger and fighting AIDS*, Action Aid. **7** UNICEF, nin.tl/UNICEFeducation **8** Nikki van der Gaag et al, *The State of the World's Girls 2014: Pathways to Power*, Plan International. **9** Nikki van der Gaag, *Feminism and Men*, Zed Books, London, 2014. **10** Gary Barker et al, *Evolving Men: Initial Results from the International Men and Gender Equality Survey* (IMAGES), International Center for Research on Women/Instituto Promundo, Washington DC/Rio de Janeiro, 2011. **11** ICRW, 'Too Young to Wed: Education and Action toward Ending Child Marriage', Brief on Child Marriage and Domestic Violence, ICRW, Washington. **12** UNESCO Ethiopia, 'Teaching and Learning: Achieving Quality for All – EFA Global Monitoring Report 2013/4. **13** Andaleeb Alam, Javier E Baez and Ximena V Del Carpio, *Does Cash for School Influence Young Women's Behavior in the Longer Term? Evidence from Pakistan*. Policy Research Working Paper 5669, World Bank, Washington, 2011. **14** UNESCO Ethiopia, op cit. and STATcompiler: Building Tables with DHS Data, ICF International, 2012. **15** Audrey Pettifor et al, 'Bed Net Ownership, Use and Perceptions Among Women Seeking Antenatal Care in Kinshasa, Democratic Republic of the Congo (DRC): Opportunities for Improved Maternal and Child Health', BMC Public Health, 2008. **16** Monazza Aslam et al, 'What works for girls' education', in *Economic Returns to Schooling and Skills: An Analysis of India and Pakistan*, RECOUP Working Paper 38, UK Department for International Development, London, 2010. **17** Katrine Saito, Hailu Mekonnen and Daphne Spurling, 'Raising the Productivity of Women Farmers in

Sub-Saharan Africa', World Bank Discussion Paper 230, Washington, 1994. **18** Jeni Klugman et al, 'Voice and Agency: Empowering Women and Girls for Shared Prosperity', World Bank, Washington, 2014. **19** Tahir Andrabi, Jishnu Das and Asim Ijaz Khwaja, 'Students Today, Teachers Tomorrow: Identifying Constraints on the Provision of Education', *Journal of Public Economics* Volume 100, April 2013. **20** UNESCO, 'Gender achievements and prospects in education', Gap report, Part One, UNICEF, 2005. **21** Nikki van der Gaag, op cit. **22** UNESCO, nin.tl/measuringICT **23** GSMA, nin.tl/GSMA-women-left-out **24** World Economic Forum, nin.tl/correcting-gap **25** GSMA, op cit. **26** GSMA, nin.tl/connected-women **27** blacklivesmatter.com **28** Nikki van der Gaag et al, *The State of the World's Girls 2010: Digital and urban frontiers*, Plan International. **29** All statistics from Center for American Progress, nin.tl/CAP-facts **30** nin.tl/indias-curse **31** IWGIA, nin.tl/gender-and-indigenous **32** The Feminist Wire, nin.tl/double-subordination **33** *The Guardian*, nin.tl/Berta-C **34** *The Guardian*, nin.tl/lola-okolosie **35** *World Report on Disability 2011*, World Bank and World Health Organization. **36** disabled world.com/disability/statistics **37** Ibid. **38** *The Guardian*, nin.tl/fem-conference **39** Ibid, and isofrida.org **40** World Bank, nin.tl/WB-disability **41** D K Marge, ed 'A call to action: preventing and intervening in violence against children and adults with disabilities: a report to the nation', in *World Report on Disability 2011*, World Bank and World Health Organization. **42** disabled-world.com/disability/statistics **43** *New Statesman,* nin.tl/NS-ryan **44** Erasing 76 Crimes, nin.tl/76-crimes **45** nin.tl/sochi-LGBT **46** *The Guardian*, nin.tl/nigeria-law **47** nin.tl/sochi-LGBT **48** European Parliament News, nin.tl/LGBT-Europe **49** *Independent*, nin.tl/SA-crisis **50** *Time*, nin.tl/2015jenner **51** *Out* magazine, nin.tl/trans-congress **52** Vanessa Baird, 'The trans revolution', *New Internationalist,* October 2015, nin.tl/trans-rev **53** Transgender Europe, nin.tl/transgender-day **54** *The Guardian*, nin.tl/trans-toilets **55** *The Advocate*, nin.tl/greer-rant **56** Feminists Fighting Transphobia, nin.tl/the-statement **57** *Ms.* magazine, nin.tl/Ms-transfeminism **58** intersexuk.org **59** *The Guardian*, nin.tl/kleeman-on-intersex **60** Vanessa Baird, op cit. **61** bell hooks, *Feminism Is for Everybody: Passionate politics*, Pluto Press, London, 2000.

3 Feminism and the Four Cs: capitalism, conflict, climate change and religious conservatism

Structural inequalities underpin the patriarchal beliefs and behaviors that threaten women. To bring about the sort of feminist revolution needed to achieve gender equality, we need to address systematic injustices rather than just focusing on individual rights.

Two steps forward, one step back?

Navigating the complexities of our world today is never easy. One the one hand, there are many who argue that feminism has now made the mainstream, particularly in the Global North. Others believe that gender equality is not only far from being realized, but that in many countries it is regressing, with women's hard-won rights under threat or even being clawed back.

This chapter looks at the place of feminism in the context of four major global challenges – capitalism and globalization, climate change, conflict and religious conservatism. It argues that all four are rooted in patriarchal beliefs and behaviors that put feminism under threat from many different directions. They also mean that feminism is uniquely placed to deal with them by collectively challenging the structural inequalities and attitudes to power that underpin them all.

Feminism co-opted?

Has feminism made the mainstream? It certainly seems like it when Beyoncé calls herself a feminist,[1] and feminism is being used to sell everything, from T-shirts to soap powder.

In her blog for the *Huffington Post*, 'Charged Up: How Big Brands Are Fueling Women's Empowerment',

Alanah Joseph notes that 'it's cool to be feminist' and scans the 'pop icons and television writers, entrepreneurs and tech executives, who are 'taking an even more noticeable stand for gender equality.' She argues: 'Corporate marketing is placing money and resources behind products and people that are empowering women, and it is making the movement more powerful.'[2]

But not everyone agrees. Critics argue that in a world increasingly dominated by the market, feminism has been co-opted by capitalism and lost its radical edge. Feminist academics have documented how gender inequality is used as a resource for global capital,[3] citing, for example, the way that companies move to the Global South where thousands of young women are prepared to work long hours for low wages and with few rights.

US critical theorist Nancy Fraser argues that 'no serious social movement, least of all feminism, can ignore the evisceration of democracy and the assault on social reproduction now been waged by finance capital'.[4]

Andi Zeisler, founder of Bitch Media,[5] argues that 'pop culture is a force that can, and has, changed the world'. In her critique of 'marketplace feminism', however, she points out that 'there are those who argue that the measure of cultural change is the degree to which that change is assimilated into existing society, those who would say that the media co-optation of a movement (say with "The Eight Best and Worst Feminists in Entertainment") is proof that it has truly made its mark'. But she also warns:

'Within a very short space of time, feminism has come to occupy perhaps its most complex role ever in American, if not global, culture... This increasingly looks not like a world that has finally emerged into fully realized feminism, but like a world in which we are letting a glossy, feel-good feminism pull focus away from deeply entrenched forms of inequality... The fight for gender equality has transmogrified from a collective goal to a consumer brand.'

Jennifer Pozner, the US founder and executive director of Women in Media & News, believes that companies are co-opting 'feminist anger at unhealthy beauty standards and media manipulations. Make no mistake: it is extremely profitable to redirect feminist energy away from media activism and toward the drugstore beauty aisle.'[6]

Although this is still largely confined to the Global North, it is not just an American phenomenon. Iliriana Banjska, who works for the Kosovo Women's Network[7] in Pristina, says: 'Young women like calling themselves "feminist", but it is more like a brand. I would love to see feminism getting more political again.'

Making the mainstream also tends to mean that ideas about 'making trouble' have been softened and simplified. According to Roxane Gray, author of *Bad Feminist*:

'So long as we continue to stare into the glittery light of the latest celebrity feminist, we avoid looking at the very real inequities that women throughout the world continue to face. We avoid having the difficult conversations about the pay gap and the all-too-often sexist music we listen to and the movies we watch that tell women's stories horribly (if at all) and the limited reproductive freedom women are allowed to exercise and the pervasive sexual harassment and violence too many women face. We avoid having the conversations about the hard work changing this culture will require.'[8]

Rachel Holmes, who co-edited *Fifty Shades of Feminism*, points out that feminism is currently being co-opted in other ways, too: 'We have never before had a situation where the rightwing military of the world's superpower is going around the world saying we are bringing feminism to liberate you; we're doing this so you can have women's basketball teams in Kabul. We have for the first time a situation where the language of feminism is being appropriated to fight wars.'[9]

The neoliberal model of capitalism, in privileging markets and competition, has also reified the individual over the collective. French philosopher Michel Foucault wrote presciently about this in the 1970s, when he said: 'The stake in all neoliberal analyses is the replacement of *homo oeconomicus* as partner of exchange with a *homo oeconomicus* as entrepreneur of himself [sic].'[10]

For feminism, this has led to a focus on the 'empowerment' of individual women and girls, reducing the problem to the individual rather than the system. It has a truly global dimension; many of the projects and programs in the Global South that focus on gender have concentrated on improving the skills, knowledge and confidence of individuals; something that is important but not enough on its own to bring about the kind of revolution that we need to achieve gender equality.

Ann Kargbo, head of an NGO in Sierra Leone, notes that women's economic empowerment must be linked to achieving gender equality. This means a fundamental challenge to the way that the economy works and who holds the power: 'We need to know who owns the resources, who controls the resources and who makes decisions on the utilization of resources.'[11]

These are the major structural barriers that prevent women's equality with men. But all too often they are ignored. They are not only about changes to the lives of individual women and girls – however important this may be. They are about who has the power to make decisions – at home, in the community, in a country and internationally – and about how those decisions are made. A feminist analysis of the real problem shows that it lies not just with individual solutions, but with a serious challenge to the structures of patriarchy.

Feminism and climate change: 3.4 billion agents of change?

Climate change and the threat it poses to our planet is one of the biggest challenges of our time. And the causes of climate change lie in the same unsustainable systems that promote inequalities, including gender inequality. This means that tackling climate change requires a transformation of our economic, political, technological and social systems. The eco-feminist movement has been making these links for some time now, as Sara Alcid notes in her blog: 'Examining environmental issues with a feminist lens enables us to see the intersection of gender, socio-economics and the environment.'[12]

Many women's organizations have recognized these key intersections as well. For example, the Women's Environmental and Development Organization (WEDO) has highlighted the links between climate change and social inequalities and has brought feminists together to take action.[13] The Women's Major Group,[14] founded in 1992 at the Earth Summit in Rio de Janeiro, Brazil, has ensured that women's groups have been able to influence the UN's policies on sustainable development and climate change. And the Women's Global Call for Climate Justice,[15] a global campaign organized by a group of regionally diverse women's rights and feminist organizations, was active at the 2015 Paris Climate Conference.

There is growing recognition that the effects of climate change are not gender-neutral, and that women and men play different roles in both mitigating and exacerbating environmental degradation.

Although gender-disaggregated data is still hard to come by, it seems clear that in many countries, marginalized women and girls are among those most affected by climate change, environmental degradation and disasters such as floods or hurricanes. This is often because their subordinate position in society means that they have less capacity and fewer resources than men to prepare for and adapt to climate change. Their family responsibilities may mean that they concentrate on protecting their children during a disaster. In the Asian tsunami in 2004, for example, this meant that more women died, particularly because many of them could not swim.[16] 'Poor women in poor countries are among the hardest hit by climate change, even though they contributed the least to it,' said former UNFPA Executive Director Thoraya Ahmed Obaid.[17]

These women are not just victims, however: they also play a major role in sustainable management of the environment that can help to prevent climate change. They are often the ones who are responsible for the family's food, energy use, waste and well-being, among other things, collecting firewood and fetching water. Although they own less land than men,[18] women farmers account for 45 to 80 per cent of all food production in developing countries[19] and are heavily involved in small-scale fishing.[20] In Southeast Asia, women provide up to 90 per cent of labor for rice cultivation. In sub-Saharan Africa they are responsible for 80 per cent of food production.[21]

As African eco-feminists noted in the run-up to the Paris climate talks in 2015: 'It is Africa's more than 500 million peasant and working-class women that carry the burden of immediate and long-term impacts of both fossil-fuel extraction and energy production, and the false solutions to the climate crisis, including corporatized renewable energy. This is because of the patriarchal-capitalist division of labor, our greater responsibility for agricultural production and social reproduction of families and communities, and our structural exclusion from decision-making.'[22]

Despite these clear gender divides, gender is generally still not a major factor when climate change is considered. Thanks to lobbying by women's and indigenous groups and others, the UN Framework Convention on Climate Change (UNFCCC) has identified adaptation, mitigation, and other issues as critical areas where gender should be considered, but only 16 per cent of countries said they take gender into account when they reported to the UNFCCC on their climate-change actions.[23] Nor do women play an equal role in climate-change negotiations, despite their expertise in environmental sustainability. In November 2013, for example, during the 19th session of the Conference of the Parties (COP), fewer than 25 per cent of official delegates were women.[24]

Because climate change is at least partly the result of a patriarchal and consumerist way of running the world, we also need to include the other half of the world – men and boys – as agents of change and activist allies alongside women. As one paper notes:

'The challenge lies in having boys and men engage in this process as a transformative step that leads away from rigid ideas of masculinity too often based on conquest, control and domination. Indeed, experts have highlighted the need to better understand how harmful ideals of masculinity that include the need to have power over others – "others" being understood as women, other men, children and nature – perpetuate environmental degradation. A gender-equitable response to climate change must not only be sensitive to gender differences in roles and needs, but must also address social and economic power imbalances between and among women and men.'[25]

If we are to tackle climate change, protect the environment, and prevent natural disasters, both men and women need to be actively involved both in their daily lives and in decision-making at all levels. 'With the possibility of a climate catastrophe on the horizon, we cannot afford to relegate the world's 3.4 billion women and girls to the role of victim,' said former UNFPA Executive Director Thoraya Ahmed Obaid. 'Wouldn't it make more sense to have 3.4 billion agents for change?'[26] Or even 7.5 billion, perhaps?

Double jeopardy: a feminist take on conflict

The ways that wars are fought have changed significantly in the past few decades. Increasingly, conflict takes place in the streets and homes of civilians, who may be used as 'human shields' against the opposing side. The result is that the percentage of civilians killed and wounded as a result of armed conflict has soared to an estimated 90 per cent today, an increasing number of whom are women and children. Women and girls are also the main victims of rape and sexual violence, used so terribly as a weapon of war in conflicts from Bosnia and Herzegovina to Rwanda. Women who are refugees also face sexual harassment and violence, as Amnesty International noted: 'Women and girl refugees face violence, assault, exploitation and sexual harassment at every stage of their journey, including on European soil.'[27]

As if the effects of conflict were not terrible enough on their own, the after-effects of war can last for many years, even generations. And the impact on gender inequalities is significant. Of the 17 countries that scored worst in the 2014 OECD Social Institutions and Gender Index (SIGI) for gender discrimination in laws, attitudes, and practices, 14 had also experienced conflict over the past two decades.[28] More than 50 per cent of the world's maternal deaths occur in conflict-affected and fragile states.[29] Both child marriage and trafficking increase.[30] The UN reports that between 2011 and 2013, eight countries reported an increase in trafficking from Syria.[31] By September 2016 there were almost five million refugees from the terrible war in Syria, where at least 125,000 people have died and

Baraa Hamid's story[32]

The scar on Baraa Hamid's back is about the size of a quarter. She has a slightly smaller one in front, near her collarbone, where a surgeon removed the sniper's bullet. She and her family were trying to flee their home town, Aleppo, to escape the fighting. She was riding in the back of a pickup truck with her mother, her brother, her brother's wife and their five children.

Hamid remembers that she couldn't speak. She remembers being afraid that her family would be shot too. They rushed her to the closest hospital, and after her surgery they fled Aleppo for the family's village in the countryside so Hamid could recuperate.

Seven months ago, they left Syria with nothing but their clothes. Now they are among the 100,000 refugees who live in this city in Turkey's hot, flat south, about an hour from the border. They live in a neighborhood where Syrians and poor Turks mingle; Syrian men walk the streets looking for odd jobs while Turkish women sit in circles, cracking walnuts to sell.

Hamid sleeps in a room with her mother and six other family members. Her brother and his wife sleep in a second bedroom. They are connected by a hallway, where they share a fridge and a small propane stove.

She rarely leaves the house – she knows no-one and does not speak Turkish. She misses her house and her friends in Aleppo, and she misses their long walks around the campus of Aleppo University.

Even before they decided to flee she had to drop out of school because her family couldn't afford the fees. 'I had a dream to finish my studies, but I couldn't,' she says. 'I would love to be in school.' She is determined to go back to Syria someday, but she knows it could take many years.

Kevin Sullivan (Washington Post)

countless more injured. Here, as always, it is often the women who are left to pick up the pieces.

Conflict also tends to increase intimate partner violence.[33] Studies in 22 countries found that women who live in fragile or conflict-affected states are a third more likely to experience violence from their partners.[34] In many countries, these women are subject to further suffering when they are ostracized or thrown out of their homes.

Women are not just passive victims; they are actively involved in times of conflict, sometimes as

Feminism

combatants, more often as peacebuilders and those who protect others and ensure that life continues. Women like 2011 Nobel Peace Laureate Leymah Gbowee, a Liberian peace activist, social worker and women's rights advocate, who brought together Christian and Muslim women to play a pivotal role in ending Liberia's civil war in 2003.[35] Or fellow Nobel prizewinner Tawakkol Karman, from Yemen, who took to the streets with thousands of other women demanding their right to freedom, justice and dignity in a nonviolent protest.[36] Women like these, together with feminist and women's organizations, are key to ending violence against women – as we will see later in this chapter.

Despite the key role women play in peacebuilding, they have been largely absent from peace negotiations. A UN study of women's participation in peace processes from 1992 to 2011 found that women make up only nine per cent of negotiating delegations, four per cent of signatories, and two per cent of chief mediators.[37] However, lobbying by women's organizations and others since 1995 has led to an increasing recognition of the importance of women's participation, and the roles they can play in speaking on behalf of marginalized groups. Rape and other forms of sexual violence have been recognized as war crimes, crimes against humanity, acts of torture, or acts associated with genocide by the international courts and tribunals for the former Yugoslavia, Rwanda and Sierra Leone, as well as the International Criminal Court. A small number of perpetrators have been successfully prosecuted.[38]

In 2000, the UN Security Council adopted the landmark Resolution 1325,[39] which recognized the need to protect the rights of women and girls during and after armed conflict, called for special measures to protect them from gender-based violence, and promoted women's roles in peacekeeping and building peace, including the need for women's leadership in peace negotiations. This was a significant move forward from previous resolutions, which only focused on women as victims. Since then, the UN Security Council has issued additional resolutions focused on sexual violence in conflict situations and involving women in peace-building and reconstruction.[40]

More recently, there has been an increasing focus on the role of masculinities in conflict. Dean Peacock of Sonke Gender Justice in South Africa[41] says: 'Whether in war or peacetime, the perpetration of sexualized violence is driven by socially sanctioned male dominance over women – and over socially weaker men, and children – by notions of manhood and power that valorize sexual conquest and give powerful men a sense of entitlement with no consequences.' Peacock concludes by saying that we need to 'demand more from our national governments, from our regional bodies and from the UN itself. We'll be far more effective in achieving this if women are not expected to end discrimination against them on their own – an impossible task. It is time for men to step forward to play their part.'

Madeleine Rees, Secretary-General of the Women's International League for Peace and Freedom (WILPF), sums up the link between feminist movements and peace movements and the goal of both: 'The global movement of feminism has a vision; it's an old one, but even more valid in our current state of the world: equality and an end to violence. It's a jigsaw as to how we get there. Each of us has to bring our pieces to the table and look up to see how they fit to build that vision into reality.'[42]

Women's rights and the rise of religious extremism

The past decade has seen a rise of extremist groups and organizations using fundamentalist approaches to religion to justify violence and attack women's rights. The Association for Women's Rights in Development (AWID) notes that 'rising fundamentalisms in many areas of the world are linked with geopolitics, systemic inequalities, militarism, displacement and other political and social factors. They have disastrous consequences for human rights, gender justice and women's equality.'[43]

In Nicaragua, María Teresa Blandón Gadea, director of feminist group La Corriente, said that they were 'really worried about the increase in religious fanaticism. We have been working with young people for years in relation to sexual and reproductive rights. And of course we realized some time ago that one of the main obstacles to talking about pleasure, virginity, sexual diversity and abortion are the religious believers.'[44]

Egyptian feminist Nawal el Saadawi believes religious extremism is pushing back on the progress that women have made and threatening the gains achieved by feminism. 'There is a backlash against feminism all over the world today because of the revival of religions,' she says.[45]

A survey by AWID found that eight out of ten women's rights activists believed religious fundamentalisms had had a negative impact on women's rights, with more than 600 examples 'manifested in the control over women's bodies, sexuality, autonomy, freedom of movement and participation in public life.[46]

This revival of ultra-conservative religion – in Islam, Christianity, Hinduism, Buddhism and Judaism – cannot be separated from other dominant global trends of globalization and increasing inequality, along with cutbacks in public services. The dispossessed and disenfranchised are turning to religion as a way to find a place in this world, or else to secure their place in the next one. Poor communities are a recruiting ground for religious groups, who may also supply the services that the state has failed to provide. A study in Somalia, for example, found that 'feeling humiliated and excluded are factors that lead young people to join or support extremist movements or violent groups'.[47]

Those who feel themselves to be at the bottom of the pile may also buy into evangelical and Pentecostal Christian 'prosperity theology', which is rife in Latin America and some countries in Africa. Linking consumerism and Christianity, its basic tenet is that, if you believe in God and support the Church, he will make you rich.

And much of this has been supported by the West, whether by fuelling extremism through external intervention, as in the case of Iraq (where the BBC's Jeremy Bowen noted: 'Iraq's perpetual war was caused by a chain of consequences that leads back to the invasion of 2003. Jihadists weren't in Iraq before the invasion'[48]), or by directly funding fundamentalist groups. As Jessica Horn notes in a report for AWID on Christian fundamentalisms in Africa: 'The most common origin of external funding is from institutions in the United States that support the growth of conservative Christianity and an ultra-conservative stance on issues of the family and sexuality.'[49]

Underpinning the fundamentalist approaches of all religions is a return to traditional ideas about gender: the belief that men are superior to women; that a woman's place is in the home, and that women need protecting, as research in four African countries found in 2006.[50] In Uganda, one church leader firmly told the researchers: 'The Bible states clearly that the woman is the priest in the home while the man is the priest in the Church. We honor them for the work they do in the home.' A Muslim woman in The Gambia said: 'We believe in the Qur'an. The Qur'an says if men are 75 per cent, then women are 25 per cent... Women are less than men. If they are equal, how come the woman leaves her home to live in the husband's home?'

Central too to fundamentalist beliefs is the exertion of control over women's bodies (see Chapter 6). This may be a gradual process, 'often beginning with dress codes, the valorization of the family and its patriarchal controls, the imposition of heterosexual "normalcy" and the regulation of marriage alliances.'[51] In Russia, for example, 'the Orthodox Church has revived stereotypes regarding women's "natural role", pushing women back into the domestic sphere. In Southeast Asia, fundamentalist interpretations of Buddhism teach boys to be leaders and girls to be servants. From Southern Baptists in the United States to militant Muslim groups in Pakistan, and in Eritrea, France, Malaysia and Serbia, religious fundamentalists seek to limit young women's access to education.'

What happens next is that religious extremist views of women and ethnic and religious minorities, of those who challenge fundamentalist movements, and of LGBTQI communities and individuals, start to be made part of the legal system in a country.

Under the Personal Status Law of 1958, Iraqi women had a number of rights. But these were replaced by the government after the 2003 US/UK-led invasion, when Islam was made the official religion and the interpretation of women's rights within law was left to religious leaders. According to Houzan Mahmoud, co-founder of the Organization of Women's Freedom in Iraq:

'The very first steps of this so-called democracy were Islamic sharia law and a Shia-Sunni divide in Iraqi society. Having an ethno-sectarian, tribalist and religious government in Iraq will only double the suffering of women, causing them to be treated as second-class citizens in society. Most policies so far have been anti-women; take the recent directive of the so-called women's minister whereby she wanted to impose "modest" clothing on women employees as another step of the Islamization of Iraq.'[52]

In Turkey, Melek Ozman, co-ordinator for the Filmmor Women's Co-operative, said: 'The influence of political

Islam is making us unable to breathe... If you ask the question, "Why is there an increase in femicide?" I would say that one of the reasons is because women are resisting against men more than they used to. Especially in the Middle Eastern region, women are demanding their emancipation. And men, on the other hand, are resisting against this and becoming more and more conservative.'[53]

The Aurat Foundation, an NGO working on women's issues in Pakistan, found that in 2014 violence against women had increased by 28 per cent over the previous year, fuelled by religious intolerance.[54]

Women like Melek and Houzan, and the organizations they work for, are part of the resistance from within their own communities to these dominant and dangerous religious ideologies. They want to promote a more progressive approach to gender within their own faiths. Sisters in Islam, from Malaysia, for example, campaigns for changes in misogynistic laws.[55] In Morocco, women have lobbied to change the religious personal statute laws; in Turkey, scholars are questioning the misogynist aspects of the *hadith* (sayings and deeds attributed to the Prophet).[56] In Togo, advocates for gender equality at community level use passages from the Bible and the Qur'an to encourage religious leaders to support gender equality.[57] And in Mali, after initial hesitation, Muslim leaders are now spreading the message that gender is a question of equality and development.[58]

Catholics for Choice campaigns on contraception, abortion and sexual and reproductive issues, based on justice and women's well-being.[59] Women Living under Muslim Laws is a network in 70 countries that has campaigned for more than 20 years to strengthen women's individual and collective struggles for equality and their rights, especially in Muslim contexts.[60] And women in the Anglican Church waged

The United Nations Development Programme (UNDP) is working with the Afghanistan Ministry of Haj and Religious Affairs to raise awareness about women's rights through capacity-development programs, scholarly competitions, advocacy, conferences and workshops. UNDP has trained religious leaders across the country about the rights of women from the perspective of Islam as well as national and international laws.

In addition to supporting publications that advocate for women's rights, activities have included student competitions, a national steering committee for women's rights, and master's degree programs to strengthen the role of government officials in campaigning for women's rights. There are also plans to arrange for religious leaders in Afghanistan to visit other Islamic countries in order to exchange knowledge with other faith leaders.

As a result of the training initiative, many Afghan religious leaders have become advocates for women's rights. A recent survey in four provinces confirms that working with faith leaders is one of the important channels for public outreach on women's rights, especially to combat gender-based violence. UNDP has also trained religious leaders on legal education – including property and land rights – and co-ordination between state and traditional justice systems.

a long campaign for female bishops, which they finally won in 2014.[62]

Young Yemeni feminist Alaa Al-Eryani, who launched a Facebook page dedicated to her country's feminist movement, says women's rights activists have to work against tough opposition – perhaps not surprising given that Yemen is at the bottom of the list of countries in the Global Gender Gap report.[63] 'I got many more negative reactions than positive ones [to my being an activist],' she says. 'I have been accused of wanting to destroy Yemeni girls: I was told that they are conservative and that I am trying to take them away from religion and traditions. These people believe it is not allowed for women to ask for their rights.'[64]

Many men, too, are standing alongside women to try to challenge religious extremism. Work with traditional and religious leaders on women's rights is seen as an increasingly important part of challenging religious extremism, as the case study on page 65 shows.

Finally, as AWID notes: 'A feminist approach is vital in addressing the nexus of development, religious fundamentalisms and women's rights; it allows one to see gender-based violence as it occurs across social levels from the state level down to the family, to understand women's bodies as a site of control for religious fundamentalists, and how this may inform policies and approaches. A feminist approach also helps us imagine ways of combating fundamentalisms that do not create further conflict, inequality or oppression.'[65]

Conclusion: joining together

Feminism is about questioning privilege and power – our own and others'. In doing so, it needs to reflect the many different situations in which women find themselves, however difficult these may sometimes be. The current state of global affairs presents many contradictory challenges for those who believe in gender equality. As Nancy Fraser says: 'Feminists [need] to join other progressive and emancipatory social movements in efforts, both intellectual and practical, to shape the direction of change.'[66] Only then can we mount a successful challenge to the patriarchal systems that drive capitalism, conflict, climate change and all forms of extremism.

1 Huffington Post, nin.tl/beyonce-feminism, and *Elle* magazine, nin.tl/change-conversation **2** Huffington Post, nin.tl/brands-and-power **3** J Acker, 'Gender, Capitalism and Globalization', *Critical Sociology 30*, 2004; M B Calas and L Smircich, "From the 'Woman's Point of View" Ten Years Later: Towards a Feminist Organization Studies', in *Handbook of Organization Studies (2nd edition)*, Sage, London, 2006. **4** Nancy Fraser, *Fortunes of Feminism: From State-Managed Capitalism to Neoliberal Crisis*, Verso, 2013. **5** Andi Zeisler, *We were* feminists once: from *Riot Grrrl* to *CoverGirl, the Buying and Selling of a Political Movement*, Public Affairs Books, 2016. **6** Identities.mic, nin.tl/10worstways **7** womensnetwork.org **8** *The Guardian,* nin.tl/lawrence-watson **9** *Guernica*, nin.tl/50-fem **10** M Foucault, *The Birth of Biopolitics: Lectures at the Collège de France, 1978-1979*. Palgrave Macmillan, New York, 2008. **11** *The Guardian,* nin.tl/unpaid-work **12** Everyday Feminism, nin.tl/feminism-valentines **13** wedo.org **14** womenmajorgroup.org **15** womenclimatejustice.org **16** John Telford, John Cosgrove, and Rachel Houghton. 'Joint evaluation of the international response to the Indian Ocean tsunami: Synthesis Report.' Tsunami Evaluation Coalition (TEC), London, 2006. **17** UNFPA, nin.tl/women-central **18** Oxfam, nin.tl/men-and-land **19** UNFPA op cit. **20** Swedish Society for Natural Conservation: *Protecting the environment: Why a gender perspective matters*, 2015. **21** Alyson Brody, Justina Demetriades and Emily Esplen, *Gender and climate change: mapping the linkages: A scoping study on knowledge and gaps*, BRIDGE, Institute of Development Studies (IDS), UK, 2008. **22** nin.tl/womin-zambia **23** Climate Change and Adaptation Research Group (CCARG) and WORLD Policy Analysis Center, Climate Adaptation Database, worldpolicyforum.org **24** *The Full Participation Report: No Ceilings*, The Bill, Hillary & Chelsea Clinton Foundation, 2015. **25** Jane Kato-Wallace et al, 'Men, Masculinities and Climate Change: A discussion paper', Men Engage Alliance, 2016. **26** UNFPA op cit. **27** Amnesty International, nin.tl/refugee-harassment **28** OECD Development Centre, Social Institutions and Gender Index 2014, available at genderindex.org; Uppsala Conflict Data Program/International Peace Research Institute (UCDP/PRIO) Armed Conflict Dataset at Uppsala University. **29** Save the Children, *State of the World's Mothers 2014: Saving Mothers and Children in Humanitarian Crises*. **30** G Lemmon, 'Fragile States, Fragile Lives: Child Marriage Amid Disaster and Conflict', Working Paper, Council on Foreign Relations, 2014, nin.tl/fragile-states; World Vision, 'Untying the Knot: Exploring Early Marriage in Fragile States', March 2013; M O'Reilly and W Alhariri, 'While Seeking Stability, Yemen Builds Momentum Against Child Marriage', *The Global Observatory*, 10 April 2014, http://theglobalobservatory. **31** UN Office on Drugs and Crime, 'Global Report on Trafficking in Persons 2014', nin.tl/2014traffickingreport **32** *The Washington Post,* nin.tl/post-refugees **33** Human Security Report Project, *Human Security Report 2012: Sexual Violence, Education, and War – Beyond the Mainstream Narrative*. **34** J Klugman and L Hanmer, 'Expanding Women's Agency: Where Do We Stand?', *Feminist Economics*. **35** Nobel Prize website, nin.tl/leymahg **36** Nobel Prize website, nin.tl/tawakkolk **37** UN Women, 'Women's Participation in Peace Negotiations: Connections between Presence and Influence', October 2012. **38** *No Ceilings: the full participation report*, The Clinton Foundation, 2015. **39** UN Security Council Resolution 1325 (October 31, 2000), UN Doc. S/RES/1325, nin.tl/res-1325 **40** B Miller, M Pournik and A Swaine, 'Women in Peace and Security through United Nations Security Resolution 1325: Literature Review, Content Analysis of National Action Plans, and Implementation', Institute for Global and International Studies, the George Washington University, May 2014. **41** When men stop fighting: Masculinities in post-conflict societies', Vienna Institute for International Dialogue and Co-operation, 31 January

2012. **42** Open Democracy, nin.tl/we-people **43** AWID, nin.tl/devil-details
44 Interview with Jean Casey, Lead Researcher and Project Co-ordinator
for *'The State of the World's Girls report 2014: Pathways to Power'*, Plan
International. **45** *The Guardian*, nin.tl/nawal-el **46** Cassandra Balchin,
Religious Fundamentalisms on the Rise: A case for action, AWID, 2008.
47 R Wolfe and J Kurtz, *Examining the Links between Youth Economic
Opportunity, Civic Engagement, and Conflict: Evidence from Mercy
Corps' Somali Youth Leaders Initiative*, Mercy Corps, 2013. **48** BBC,
nin.tl/iraqinvasion **49** Jessica Horn, *Christian Fundamentalisms and
Women's Rights in the African Context: Mapping the Terrain,* AWID, 2010.
50 Senhorina Wendoh and Tina Wallace, 'Living Gender in African Organ-
isations and Communities: Stories from The Gambia, Rwanda, Uganda
and Zambia', Transform Africa, 2006. **51** Bina Srinivasan, *Religious funda-
mentalism, community disintegration, and violence against women: All
issues are women's issues*, Socialism and Democracy, 2004. **52** Equality in
Iran, theoccupiedtimes.org/?p=2860 **53** Sisterhood, nin.tl/stemming-tide
54 *Daily Times,* nin.tl/surge-in-attacks **55** sistersinislam.org.my **56** *The
Guardian*, nin.tl/islamicfem **57** Leslie M Fox, Fatou Jah, and Andrew
John Howe, 'Cross- Country Research Study on: Access of Girls and
Women to Decision-Making Processes in West Africa and Cameroon',
Research commissioned for the 'Because I am a Girl Report.' Plan
International West Africa Regional Office, 2014. **58** Plan International,
'Case Study 1: The Creation of a National Gender Policy in Mali.' Plan
West Africa Office, 2013. **59** catholicsforchoice.org **60** wluml.org/
node/5408 **61** UNDP, nin.tl/leaders-support **62** BBC, nin.tl/CofE-bishops
63 World Economic Forum, nin.tl/WEFgap2015 **64** The Voice of Yemen,
nin.tl/yemeni-feminist **65** AWID, nin.tl/devil-details **66** *The New York
Times opinionator,* nin.tl/lean-in-lean-on

4 You can keep a good woman down: power, politics and privilege

The barriers that are holding women back are also holding back global economic development. Yet from care work to teaching, from farming to factory work, women continue to face discrimination in the labor market, despite claims to the contrary. Could it be that capitalism can only function if such inequalities continue?

Introduction: is the tide turning?

One of the many arguments levelled against feminism, by both women and men, is that we no longer need it – at least in the Global North. While most people recognize that we are a long way from gender equality in countries such as Afghanistan or Saudi Arabia, they believe that women in the 'rich world' should stop complaining. They already have it all, so this case goes, particularly when it comes to the world of work.

Some go even further. Hanna Rosin, in her book *The End of Men*, believes that, in the US at least, 'the tides have turned. The "age of testosterone" is decisively over. At almost every level of society women are proving themselves far more adaptable and suited to a job market that rewards people skills and intelligence, and a world that has a dramatically diminishing need for traditional male muscle.'[1] She even goes so far as to say: 'The modern economy is becoming a place where women hold the cards.'

Her evidence for this is that, for the first time ever, women in the US hold just over half the jobs[2] and that more women than men are in further education. Further afield, she cites the fact that women own more than 40 per cent of private businesses in China, and that there are women leaders like Jóhanna Sigurðardóttir, who, as Prime Minister of Iceland between 2009 and

2013, was the world's first openly lesbian head of state.

If we look at the facts globally, it is true that women are entering the paid workforce in greater numbers and that we have more women leaders than ever before. This is something to celebrate. But look a little more closely, and the picture is rather less clear. First, there is the overall economic context: 29 million net jobs were lost during the global economic crisis in 2012 and many of these have not been recovered.[3] And austerity measures following the 2007-8 financial crisis led to cutbacks in services, the burden of which falls largely on women and girls.

The International Labour Organization says that while the gender gap in labor-force participation rate decreased from 27.9 to 26.1 per cent in the 1990s, it has remained the same in the decade from 2002 to 2012. In three regions – East Asia, South Asia and Central and Eastern Europe – the gender gap in employment participation actually increased.[4]

In the Global North, women's employment in industry has halved, so that 85 per cent now work in services, primarily education and health, traditionally seen as 'soft' areas and thus suitable for females. In the Global South, women moved out of agriculture, and into services, with the exception of East Asia, where 25 per cent of women are now employed in industry.[5]

Of course, women, especially poor women, have always had to work, whether for money or not, and this kind of work – informal, often badly paid, insecure – is not always something to be celebrated.

In South Asia, sub-Saharan Africa and East and Southeast Asia (excluding China), more than 75 per cent of all jobs are informal. In rural areas, much of this is through small-scale farming, where there is often little or no pay.[6] The vast majority (83 per cent) of the 53 million domestic workers are women – including many migrant workers, with little pay and fewer rights.

Women are also still paid less than men for the same work – globally, women earn on average 24 per cent less than men, and where this gap has narrowed, it is often because wages have fallen for men as well, which is hardly something to be celebrated.

Certain groups of women, particularly those who are marginalized, have an even bigger gender gap in their pay. In the US, women on average have to work for 15 months to earn what a man earns in 12. But if you are a Black or Native American woman, this rises to between 20 and 22 months. Transgender women, too, are four times more likely than the rest of the population to have a household income of under $10,000 a year.[7]

The gender pay gap also varies considerably according to the kind of job you do. Claudia Goldin, Harvard University labor economist and a specialist on women and the economy, found that in a few professions, women and men in the US earn the same, but in others there is a definite gap. Female doctors and surgeons only earn 71 per cent of a male wage, while nurses earn 91 per cent.[8]

Perhaps none of this is surprising given that, in many countries, men (and some women) still believe in the idea of the man-as-breadwinner, despite the reality often being very different. A survey by the Pew Research Center[9] found that, when asked to agree or disagree with the statement 'When jobs are scarce, men should have more right to a job', there was a huge variation between countries, with 84 per cent of respondents in India agreeing with the statement, compared with 49 per cent in Russia, 41 per cent in Brazil, 14 per cent in the US, and 12 per cent in Britain and Spain. In some countries, men were much more likely than women to agree – in Egypt, for example, 90 per cent of men but only 60 per cent of women agreed.[10]

The changes in women's relationship to the labor force are happening at the same time as globalization and privatization in the service of a worldwide neoliberal agenda that favors the market over everything else.

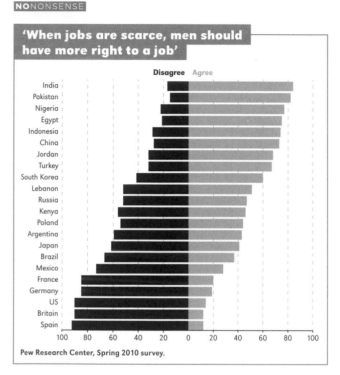

'When jobs are scarce, men should have more right to a job'

Disagree   Agree

India
Pakistan
Nigeria
Egypt
Indonesia
China
Jordan
Turkey
South Korea
Lebanon
Russia
Kenya
Poland
Argentina
Japan
Brazil
Mexico
France
Germany
US
Britain
Spain

100   80   60   40   20   0   20   40   60   80   100

Pew Research Center, Spring 2010 survey.

As Stephanie Coontz, Professor of Family History at Evergreen State College in the US, points out:

'Social and economic policies constructed around the male breadwinner model have always disadvantaged women. But today they are dragging down millions of men as well. Paradoxically, putting gender-equity issues at the center of social planning would now be in the interests of most men... It's the best way to reverse the increasing economic vulnerability of men and women alike. Given the increasing insecurity of many American men, they have good reason to back feminist policies.'[11]

Free-trade zones in countries like Bangladesh have brought employment to thousands of young women who

Feminism

otherwise would probably have stayed at home. They constitute 80 per cent of the 4.2 million people who work in the garment export industry.[12] Bringing an income to their families gives them status and more independence than they might otherwise have had, as social economist Naila Kabeer points out.[13] But they also have few rights and are paid very little for their labor.

Women on top?

At the other end of the spectrum, women are still struggling to break the glass ceiling, despite some improvements. Things have changed shockingly little when it comes to women in powerful positions, and in some cases have even gone backwards. Many of the statistics below are from the so-called 'rich world':

- In 2016, there were only 21 female CEOs running Fortune 500 companies – down from 24 in 2014.[14]
- Less than one in four senior management roles globally are held by women (24 per cent). This is unchanged from 2007.

Ei Yin Mon's story, Burma[15]

'I arrived in Rangoon after Cyclone Nargis in 2008 because there were no jobs after the cyclone. I wanted to be a schoolteacher, but failed Year 10 and had to start working to support my family. My sister and I support our youngest sister, who is still in high school, and send money home to my mother, who has diabetes and heart problems.

'I don't want to keep working at the factory because the base wage is so low and we are pressured to do long hours of overtime. We are always being told to work faster. They think that we are like animals. I know I have no rights to make a complaint, so I have to bear it. I have been working here so many years and we try our best to meet the production targets so that we won't be told off, but sometimes it [the yelling] is unbearable.

'We once had an accident and there was a fire in the factory. At that time, people were shouting at us to turn off the main switch. But we didn't know how to turn it off. We hadn't received any training or information about safety.'

- In the European Union, women make up only 16.6 per cent of board members of large publicly listed companies. One in four big companies still have no women on the board.
- In the Netherlands, women make up only 10 per cent of the boards of the top 100 companies. In Britain, the figure is 20.7 per cent.
- In OECD countries, women earn on average 16 per cent less than men, but female top-earners are paid 21 per cent less than their male counterparts
- In addition, even though the percentage has almost doubled since 1995, still less than a quarter of parliamentarians globally are women.[16]

Apart from Sweden and Finland, the countries with the highest percentage of women in parliament might come as a surprise (see below). Rwanda's success is largely due to a decision to have a 50-per-cent quota for women in parliament. There is much criticism of quotas, but they can be an effective temporary measure to get women to the top, whether in parliament or elsewhere. For example, Norway has pioneered the quota approach to bringing women into the boardroom and now has 40-per-cent female representation at board level.[17]

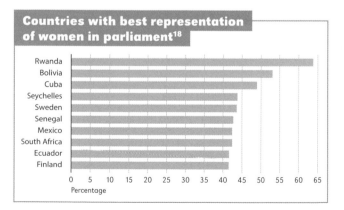

Countries with best representation of women in parliament[18]

Feminism

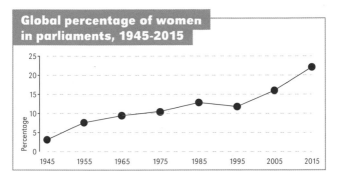

Global percentage of women in parliaments, 1945-2015

And what about other countries of the Global North, where women are educated and, according to Hanna Rosin, 'hold all the cards'? Britain ranks just 48th, with 29.4 per cent. The US fares even worse, in 97th position, with 19.4 per cent. Despite wealth, democracy and women's education, these countries are still overwhelmingly ruled by men.

And this is also true if we look at management positions in private companies. Interestingly, women hold a similar proportion of senior roles here to their share of parliamentary seats. The latest report from Grant Thornton International shows that, in 2015, 24 per cent of senior roles globally were held by women, up from 22 per cent in 2015 and the same as 2014. But a third of businesses still have no women in senior management positions, although this varies quite widely from country to country.[19]

If we start to dig deeper, moreover, we find that these figures once again vary hugely according to the color of your skin. The chart overleaf, based on research from the American Association of University Women, shows that both employment itself and the percentage of people in senior positions favor white men over white women, but also hugely disadvantage those from other backgrounds. This is true in many other spheres as well – of the 98 women in Congress, only 14 are African American women.[20]

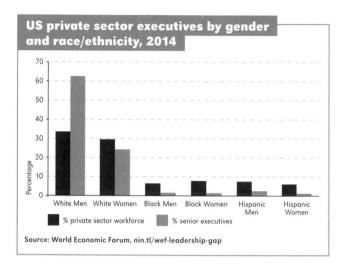

US private sector executives by gender and race/ethnicity, 2014

Source: World Economic Forum, nin.tl/wef-leadership-gap

Unpaid care work: a feminist issue

One of the things preventing women gaining equality with men at work – whether as CEO, factory worker or farmer – is the fact that, as well as doing their paid work, they are also doing between two and ten times[21] more unpaid work and childcare and, increasingly, care for the old, than men.

This means that millions of women are effectively doing two jobs at once: one paid and one unpaid. In addition to holding them back at work, this underpins unequal power relations, is a barrier to education, and reinforces stereotypes about women's and men's roles and position in society. It affects most the poorest women and those who are marginalized by class, caste or ethnicity, as they cannot afford to pay for childcare and are more likely to live in areas where there are few public services.[22]

'It is hard to think of a human right that is not potentially affected in some way by the unequal distribution and difficulty of unpaid care work,' wrote Magdalena Sepúlveda Carmona, UN Special

Sad truths: women and diversity in the US media[23]

Despite high-profile campaigns for more women in the media – for example, by the movie star Geena Davis[24] – things have shifted surprisingly little. A 2015 report from the Women's Media Center[25] revealed:

1 **The news industry still hasn't achieved gender equality.** Women were on camera only 32 per cent of the time in evening broadcast news, and wrote 37 per cent of print news stories. Between 2013 and 2014, female bylines and other credits increased by just over one per cent. At the *New York Times*, more than 67 per cent of bylines were male.

2 **Men still dominate 'hard news'.** Men reported 65 per cent of political stories, 63 per cent of science stories, 64 per cent of world politics stories and 67 per cent of criminal justice news. Women lost traction in sports journalism, with only 10 per cent of sports coverage produced by women (in 2014 it was 17 per cent). Education and lifestyle coverage were the only areas that demonstrated any real parity.

3 **Opinions are apparently a male thing.** Newspaper editorial boards were on average made up of seven men and four women. And 70 per cent of commentators on Sunday morning talk-shows were male.

4 **Hollywood executives are still overwhelmingly white and male.** Ninety-two per cent of studio senior management were white, and 83 per cent were male.

5 **Women and Black and minority groups are still largely absent.** Women accounted for only 12 per cent of on-screen protagonists in 2014, and only 30 per cent of characters with speaking parts. There were also persistent racial disparities: white people were cast in lead roles more than twice as often as people of color, and white film writers outnumbered minority writers three to one. In 17 per cent of films, no black people had speaking parts.

6 **Women are losing traction behind the scenes.** Women accounted for 25 per cent of writers in 2013-14, down from 34 per cent the previous year. Women made up only 23 per cent of executive producers (down from 27 per cent). For the 250 most profitable films made in 2014, 83 per cent of the directors, producers, writers, cinematographers and editors were men.

There has been some progress. At the *Chicago Sun-Times*, 54 per cent of the bylines were female, and 53 per cent of contributors to the *Huffington Post* were women.

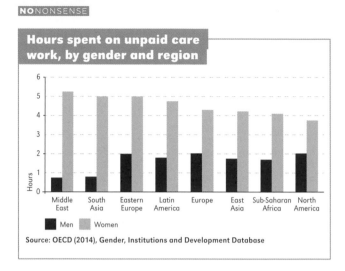

Hours spent on unpaid care work, by gender and region

Hours

■ Men   ■ Women

Source: OECD (2014), Gender, Institutions and Development Database

Rapporteur on extreme poverty and human rights. 'Millions of women still find that poverty is their reward for a lifetime spent caring, and unpaid care provision by women and girls is still treated as an infinite cost-free resource that fills the gaps when public services are not available or accessible.'[26]

Without this unpaid care work, however, our economies and societies would not be able to function, as feminist economist Corina Rodríguez Enríquez has pointed out.[27] Yet it remains both invisible and unvalued, both socially and in monetary terms, despite the fact that it has been estimated to be worth between 10 and 50 per cent of most countries' gross domestic product (GDP).[28]

Unpaid care work is slowly beginning to be recognized, with a focus on recognition, reduction and redistribution.[29] The United Nations' Sustainable Development Goals (SDGs) have a specific target on unpaid care work under Goal Five: Achieve gender equality and empower all women and girls.[30]

But the issue of unpaid care work has not been at the forefront of the feminist agenda, perhaps at least

Feminism

partly because women are reluctant to give up power in the one place where they have it: the home. It is undoubtedly a feminist issue, and one that goes beyond individual change. Solving the problem of unpaid care work, especially with an ageing population that will need looking after, involves many structural changes – for example, ensuring easier access to clean water, quality education, social protection, healthcare and childcare services. It also means men stepping up to the plate and taking on their fair share of this work, rather than just 'helping out' or being praised for 'babysitting' their own children.[31]

This will involve huge changes in employment practices – among others, more flexible working for all, parental leave, and workplace childcare. As Sheryl Sandberg, CEO of Facebook, said: 'It has been more than two decades since I entered the workforce, and so much is still the same. It is time for us to face the fact that our revolution has stalled. The promise of equality is not the same as true equality. A truly equal world would be one where women ran half our countries and companies and men ran half our homes.'[32] Yet research in Britain of more than five million job advertisements found that less than nine per cent of vacancies for decently paid jobs in the UK offer flexible working.[33]

What might this mean in practice for poor women? A World Bank study in 20 countries found that although there was growing acceptance that women have a productive role to play in the paid workforce, this was still seen as being on top of their unpaid responsibilities at home. One men's group in Nsenene village, Tanzania, for example, felt that in addition to traditional care duties, the tasks of a 'good wife' were: 'She does all the cleaning. She prepares breakfast. She works on the plantation in the morning. She prepares lunch. She goes to work on the plantation in the afternoon. She attends association meetings in the late afternoon. She comes back to make sure supper is ready. She serves supper. She goes to bed and should have sex with her husband.'[34]

An Action Aid project[35] in Nepal, Nigeria, Uganda and Kenya focused on women's unpaid care work with the aim of making it both more visible and more valued by women and men, community leaders and government. A woman from rural Uganda explained how things had changed for her: 'I used to carry two hoes, one for myself and the other for my husband, whenever we would go and come back from the garden, but now he carries his own hoe and when we get back home he helps me take care of the children. For instance, sometimes he bathes them and takes them to sleep as I do other housework like washing of dishes and cooking.'

Other campaigns, such as MenCare, are pushing for men to become more involved in childcare and work in the home, arguing that this will mean more women working for pay outside the home: 'The fact that women do most of the care work is one of the key reasons that women's wages are lower than men's, even when they work in the same kinds of jobs.'[36]

Leaning in and leaning out

So what can feminists do to ensure that women have equality at work? Many of the solutions proposed in the Global North have tended to point the finger at women themselves, or to blame individuals for the lack of any real and sustainable change.

For example, Linda Babcock and Sarah Laschever[37] blame the lack of progress on women's lack of confidence; women are less likely than men, they say, to negotiate pay or conditions. Sheryl Sandberg caused huge controversy in 2013 with her book *Lean In: women, work and the will to lead*, in which she talked about the ways 'women are hindered by barriers that exist within ourselves'.

Despite – or perhaps because – of the controversy and the huge amount of publicity the book generated,

Lean In has gone viral. There is a website (leanin.org) and 27,000 'circles' in countries from China to Iraq. Carrie Huang, aged 21, from China, says: 'My friends and I... we underestimate ourselves. It has to do with our education and background. Our parents tell us, "You are girls; get yourself a stable life and don't have too much ambition." We lack confidence.' Many women in China prioritize their boyfriends' or husbands' goals, Huang says. 'What we need is the courage to try different things. It's about discovering what you want to do.'[38]

This approach can help individual women improve their chances at work, but is it necessarily a feminist project? Not all women in senior positions champion gender equality; some may even do the opposite. Dawn Foster, British author of *Lean Out*[39] wrote in *The Guardian*:

'The problem with corporate feminism's obsession with individual stories of success, and "having it all", is that many women don't have much at all. Women have been disproportionately affected by austerity, with single mothers and pensioners particularly affected. A few more women may be MPs or CEOs, but three times as many young women are locked into low-paid jobs than they were 20 years ago. The fall in real-term wages affects women more, since they were earning less in the first place. Asking women to "lean in" is far easier than demanding we fundamentally change the way businesses operate, and how we reward and approach work.'[40]

In any case, women have always come together in order to bring about or demand change. It is largely due to women's organizations all over the world that we have come as far as we have. Collective action for change, including through trade unions, has brought about changes in legislation on employment – and ensured that it is enforced. Women have campaigned for a variety of employment rights, for flexible

Women organizing in informal employment

- Women in Informal Employment Globalizing and Organizing (WIEGO) is a global network. It has raised the visibility of informal workers on the international stage and helped to improve conditions nationally. For example, WIEGO supported HomeNet Thailand to advocate for a law for Thailand's two million homeworkers that ensures wages are protected, provides for occupational health and safety, and makes employers legally responsible.[41]
- Via Campesina is made up of over 160 grassroots organizations representing peasants, smallholders, agricultural workers, migrants, youth, indigenous groups and landless people in more than 70 countries. After a long struggle, women today hold senior positions and are a central force in the movement.[42]
- The Self-Employed Women's Association (SEWA) in India has almost two million members. It provides savings and credit, health and childcare, insurance, legal aid and capacity building, as well as supporting members in negotiations with employers. For example, SEWA Delhi, in partnership with the UK-based Ethical Trading Initiative (ETI), negotiated for companies to buy directly from home-based workers rather than through intermediaries. This meant that sub-contracted workers could become self-employed, form their own producer group, and negotiate better rates.[43]
- In Brazil, the Domestic Workers' Federation (FENATRAD) has helped to bring about legal reforms to advance the rights of the country's seven million domestic workers.[44]

working, affordable childcare and social protection. Even in areas where it is most difficult, for example the millions of women who work in informal employment, they have had many successes (see box).

The feminist agenda, then, has to be for changes to attitudes and behaviors among both men and women, but also in government policies and business practices. Good and affordable childcare, shared parenting, flexible working, equal pay, parental leave, a living wage for all, improved welfare benefits and unemployment insurance, as well as support and mentoring for women in the workplace, are among the many things that are needed for change to happen.

Feminism

Myrtle Witbooi became a domestic worker in 1966 when she wasn't allowed to go on to further education. She served one family for 12 years, raising their child with love, working without even one paid holiday.

In 1969, when a newspaper article disparaged domestic workers for bad behavior, she made her voice heard in a letter to the editor, demanding: 'Why are we different? Why must we work like slaves?'

This spontaneous outburst changed her life forever. She was invited by a journalist to organize a meeting for domestic workers, and 250 people turned up. Myrtle stood before them, incredibly nervous, never having addressed a group of that size. It took until 2000 for them to form a union of their own: the South African Domestic, Service and Allied Workers Union (SADSAWU).

'We had been slaves; now we had a union,' Myrtle explains. 'We did the bulk of the work passing the domestic-worker labor laws in South Africa.' When the discussion on standards for domestic workers was put on the agenda of the International Labour Conference, SADSAWU, with other domestic workers' unions and associations, agreed to mobilize worldwide support. They established the International Domestic Workers' Network, and Myrtle was asked to be president.

Myrtle speaks with the same passion and commitment that prompted her to write that first letter four decades ago: 'It is in the solidarity that we now have that we find we share one common goal; to free ourselves from slavery, to be recognized as human beings. We want to be seen as women who do a decent job, adding to the economy of the world, enriching it. There is a slogan in South Africa that women won't be free until domestic workers are free. What we mean by that is that until my employer sees me as a human being, a woman that other women respect, domestic workers won't be free. We want it to come in our lifetime.'

Conclusion: 100 years to go?

Even from a neoliberal point of view, there are few arguments for not pushing a feminist agenda. In monetary terms alone, the International Labour Organization points out that the barriers which hold back women 'also hold back economic growth and development in countries with large gender gaps.'[46]

A McKinsey Global Institute report[47] puts a figure on this – it finds that $12 trillion could be added to global GDP by 2025 by advancing women's equality. In India, 'gender equality would have a larger economic impact than in any other region in the world – $700 billion of added GDP in 2025', but for this to happen, comprehensive change is needed, including 'raising women's participation in India's labor force by 10 percentage points between now and 2025, bringing 68 million more women into the labor force. This will require bridging both economic and social gender gaps.'[48]

The OECD reports that if women in the US worked at the same rates as men, GDP could grow by nine per cent; in France by more than 11 per cent; and in Italy by 23 per cent. On average, across OECD countries, if women's participation in the workplace were to converge with men's rates by 2030, we could see an overall increase of 12 per cent in GDP.[49]

Price Waterhouse Cooper's annual Women in Work Index shows that Britain could boost its GDP by nine per cent, or £170 billion ($217 billion), if it could increase the percentage of women in work to match that of Sweden.[50]

Business leaders argue consistently for the benefits of diversity. Francesca Lagerberg from Grant Thornton says that 'businesses with diverse workforces can outperform their more homogeneous peers and are better positioned to adapt to a rapidly changing global business environment.'[51] Fortune 500 companies with the highest representation of women board directors attained significantly higher financial performance, on average, than those with the lowest representation of women board directors.[52]

Despite all this evidence, a 2016 report by McKinsey[53] puts the final nail in the coffin of the idea that women are having it all in the workplace – it reckons that we are at least 100 years away from equality.

Small wonder that some women see feminism as not just aiming to redress inequality in the workplace but rather challenging capitalism itself. As Amit Singh writes:

'Feminism has historically been about eradicating and opposing inequality. Feminism is thus incompatible with capitalism, as this is a system that compounds and exacerbates such inequality. It is, simply put, a system that requires inequality for it to thrive and function effectively. Earning a lot of money won't eradicate these inequalities, it will exacerbate them, as people around the world will continue to live in incredible impoverishment and harsh conditions.'[54]

In the end, it doesn't matter whether gender equality is good for wealth creation. It's a matter of basic justice.

The UN High Level Panel on Women's Economic Empowerment noted in September 2016: 'Women's economic empowerment is not limited to decent employment and income for women. It requires removing barriers in the market and public institutions to redistribute women's unpaid care, deliver women's security and agency, recognizing that social norms primarily limit what is considered women's work and their role in society.'[55]

We can only hope that our granddaughters are as horrified about the situation of women in the workplace today as we are about the fact that women couldn't vote 100 years ago.

1 UN Women, *Progress of the World's Women 2015-2016: Transforming Economies, Realizing Rights*, New York, 2015. **2** US Department of Labor, nin. tl/usdl-data **3** Global employment trends for women, Executive Summary, 2012, International Labour Organization. **4** Ibid. **5** Ibid. **6** *Progress of the World's Women 2015-2016*, op cit. **7** Feministing, nin.tl/pay-cisgender **8** *New York Times*, nin.tl/gender-not-jobs **9** Pew Global, nin.tl/men-have-edge **10** Pew Global, nin.tl/July2010report **11** Stephanie Coontz, nin.tl/helping-women **12** *Progress of the World's Women 2015-2016*, op cit. **13** N Kabeer, *The Power to Choose: Bangladeshi Women and Labour Market Decisions in London and Dhaka*, Verso, London, 2000. **14** Fortune, nin.tl/2015-bad-year **15** D Gardner J Burnley, *Made in Myanmar*. Quoted in Francesca Rhodes et al, 'Underpaid and undervalued, how inequality defines women's work in Asia', Oxfam Issue Briefing, Oxfam International, 2016. **16** ipu.org/wmn-e/world.htm **17** The Conversation, nin.tl/norwaylessons **18** IPU, nin.tl/women-in-parliament **19** *Women in business: turning promise into practice*, Grant Thornton International Business Report 2016. **20** Center for American Progress, nin.tl/cap-report **21** Gaëlle Ferrant et al, *Unpaid Care Work: The missing link in the analysis of gender gaps in labour outcomes*, OECD Development Centre, 2014. **22** sustainabledevelopment.un.org/?menu=1300 **23** *Time*, nin.tl/sadtruths **24** seejane.org **25** *Time*, nin.tl/sadtruths **26** Carmona M Sepúlveda, Report of the Special Rapporteur on Extreme Poverty and Human Rights: Unpaid Care Work and Women's Human Rights, United Nations, 2013. **27** Corina Rodríguez Enríquez, *Care: the missing link in economic analysis?* Cepal Review 106, April 2012. **28** An UNRISD study of six countries estimated 10 to 39 per cent (see Debbie Budlender, 'The statistical evidence on care and non-care work across six countries', UNRISD, Gender and Development Programme Paper No 4, December 2008), but measurements in different countries have been even higher. Estimates for 2009-10 in Australia suggest that the amount of unpaid care work undertaken was around 21.4 billion hours, equivalent to 50.6 per cent of GDP (SA Hoenig and ARE Page, *Counting on Care Work in Australia*, report prepared by AEC Group Limited for economic Security4Women, Australia, 2012). **29** First defined by Diane Elson at a UNDP workshop and later included in A Fälth & M Blackden, 'Unpaid 10. Care Work', Gender Equality and Poverty Reduction, Issue 1. UNDP, New York, 2009. **30** sustainabledevelopment.un.org/?menu=1300 **31** Unpaid Care Platform, Men Care, 2016. **32** Lean In, nin.tl/sandberg-to-grads **33** *The Guardian*, nin.tl/flexi-jobs **34** Ana Maria Munoz Boudet, Patti Petesch, and Carolyn Turk with Angelica Thumala, '*On Norms and Agency Conversations about Gender Equality with Women and Men in 20 Countries*', World Bank 2012. **35** actionaid.org/unpaidcarework **36** Men Care, nin.tl/10-mencare-themes **37** Linda Babcock and Sarah Laschever, *Women Don't Ask: Negotiation and the Gender Divide*, Berkeley Books, 2003. **38** *New York Times*, nin.tl/chinafeminism **39** Dawn Foster, *Lean Out*, Repeater Books, London, 2016. **40** *The Guardian*, nin.tl/corporatefeminism **41** wiego.org/wiego-in-brief/selected-impact-stories **42** *Progress of the World's Women 2015- 2016*, op cit. **43** Ibid. **44** Ibid. **45** Adapted from 'Our Struggle Is far From Over' by Leslie Tuttle, nin.tl/myrtles-story **46** Global Employment Trends for Women 2012, ILO, Geneva, nin.tl/GETforwomen **47** McKinsey & Company, nin.tl/mckinseyequality **48** Ibid. **49** oecd.org/gender/ **50** PWC, nin.tl/women-in-work2016 **51** *Women in business: turning promise into practice*, Grant Thornton International Business Report 2016 **52** Why Diversity Matters, Catalyst Information Center, 2013. **53** McKinsey & Co, nin.tl/gender-challenge **54** New Internationalist blog, nin.tl/cap-fem-pay **55** UN, nin.tl/WEEreport

5 Violence against women: a never-ending epidemic

Violence – and the threat of it – prevents women from playing an equal role in society. And it continues to be shockingly common. There are many prevention strategies, but as it is mainly men who use violence against women, working with them has to be part of the feminist project to stop the violence and break the patriarchal system behind it.

Introduction: keeping safe?

Most women and girls will, on some occasion, have hesitated to walk down a dark street alone, or glanced behind them because of footsteps that sound too close.

Despite decades of campaigning by women's organizations, and an increase in legislation – almost 120 countries have laws on domestic violence, 125 have laws on sexual harassment and 52 have laws on marital rape – violence against women and girls continues unabated. It cuts across race, class and geography. It is not only marginalized men from the poorest communities who assault their wives and girlfriends; bankers and billionaires do it too. Violence doesn't just make women afraid; it also prevents them from playing an equal role in society. So if we are to have an equal world, ending violence needs to be high on the feminist agenda.

In September 2016, the media was full of Brock Turner, the US student who sexually assaulted an unconscious woman and was given only a six-month sentence. Turner's father said his son should not have to go to prison for '20 minutes of action'. The judge said the leniency of the sentence was the result of his age, his lack of a criminal history, the role that alcohol played in the assault, and good character references. 'A prison sentence would have a severe impact on him,' said the

What is violence against women?

The 1993 United Nations Declaration on the Elimination of Violence against Women (Article 1) was the first internationally agreed definition. It states that violence against women 'means any act of gender-based violence that results in, or is likely to result in, physical, sexual or psychological harm or suffering to women, including threats of such acts, coercion or arbitrary deprivation of liberty, whether occurring in public or in private life.'[1]

In 1995, the Beijing Platform at the UN Fourth World Conference on Women extended this to include 'dowry-related violence, marital rape, female genital mutilation and other traditional practices harmful to women, non-spousal violence and violence related to exploitation, including rape, sexual abuse, sexual harassment and intimidation at work, in educational institutions and elsewhere, trafficking in women and forced prostitution; and physical, sexual and psychological violence perpetrated or condoned by the State.[2]

judge. 'I think he will not be a danger to others.'[3]

The lenient sentence caused a media outcry, with 400,000 people signing a petition demanding that the judge be removed from office. 'This sentence is making all women at Stanford less safe, because it is sending a message to women students that says: "If this happens to you, you are on your own,"' said Michelle Dauber, a professor at the university.[4]

Turner's victim wrote a moving letter to him in which she explained what she went through after the assault (which she does not remember): 'I used to pride myself on my independence. Now I am afraid to go on walks in the evening, to attend social events with drinking among friends where I should be comfortable being... You bought me a ticket to a planet where I lived by myself. Every time a new article came out, I lived with the paranoia that my entire hometown would find out and know me as the girl who got assaulted. I didn't want anyone's pity and am still learning to accept victim as part of my identity... And finally, to girls everywhere, I am with you. On nights when you feel alone, I am with you. When people doubt you or dismiss you, I am with you... never stop fighting, I believe you.'[10]

What happened to her still happens to women and girls every day in every country in the world, but we don't usually hear about it. The terrible rape and death of a young woman in Delhi, in India, was one other story that did make the headlines and led to huge protests. Over a decade, hundreds of women were abducted, raped and murdered in and around Ciudad Juarez, Mexico.[11] It is estimated that, worldwide, one in five women will be a victim of rape or attempted rape, more often than not by a man that they know.[12]

Despite these figures, even some of those who work on gender and support women's rights dismiss the statistics as 'something everyone knows'. The term 'domestic violence' somehow reduces it to the mundane, and 'intimate partner violence' sounds somehow 'safe' and contained. Perhaps the horror is just too hard to contemplate, or the statistics have been repeated so many times that they no longer have the power to shock. But until both the statistics and the stories are given the sustained attention they deserve – the kind of attention that leads to action – women and girls will continue to feel unsafe in their own homes, in the street, at work, or in any other place where they should be free from fear.

> ### Girls' attitudes to violence and sexual harassment in Britain[13]
>
> A 2015 survey by Girlguiding of 1,574 girls between 7 and 21 found high levels of concern about violence and sexual harassment. Three-quarters said anxiety about sexual harassment negatively affected their lives – from choice of clothing (51 per cent), to body confidence (49 per cent) or freedom to go where they want on their own (43 per cent). A significant minority of girls aged 13 to 21 said that their partner had displayed controlling or coercive behavior. Two in three young women (67 per cent) agreed that popular culture tells boys that they are entitled to coerce or abuse their girlfriends.

Violence and patriarchal thinking

In many countries, patriarchal thinking means that men – and some women – still believe violence is acceptable. For example, the World Values survey from 2010 to 2014 found that although two-thirds of men said that beating your wife was 'never justifiable', in 29 countries, between 30 and 50 per cent thought that it was.[14] Perhaps more surprisingly, in 19 countries, one in three women also agreed that a husband who beats his wife may sometimes be justified.

A UN study of 10,000 men in Bangladesh, Cambodia, China, Indonesia, Sri Lanka and Papua New Guinea found that men cited their right to have sex whether the woman agreed to or not as the most common reason for rape.[15]

In Colombia, where one woman is reportedly killed by her partner or former partner every six days,[16] a government report on public tolerance for violence against women found that 37 per cent of respondents thought that 'real men can control their women' and 18 per cent believed that 'a good wife should obey her husband'.[17]

A survey in the European Union found that on average more than half of men and women agreed that women's provocative behavior was a cause of domestic violence against women.[18] In Russia, a study in Karelia found that 21 per cent of men 'fully agreed or agreed' that if a woman was raped, it meant that she had behaved frivolously and therefore had got herself into the situation. One third of men 'fully agreed or agreed' that sometimes women want to be raped.[19]

In some countries, however, attitudes are changing, perhaps because of legislation or media campaigns, and because women and girls are becoming more aware of their rights. In Nigeria, for example, 44 per cent of women said in 2003 that it was okay for a husband to beat his wife, but 10 years later this figure had dropped to 21 per cent. In Benin, the decline during the same period was from 39 to 10 per cent; in Haiti, from 11 to 3 per cent.[20] So perhaps there is some reason for hope.

One of the retorts that is often given is that women are also violent, and that the focus should therefore not just be on violence perpetrated by men. But although women are sometimes violent, the vast majority of violence against men is perpetrated by other men, not by women. Neither are violent and abusive women supported by a whole culture that finds violence and abuse by men, and misogyny, acceptable. A study published by the American Society of Criminology found that men make up almost 80 per cent of violent offenders reported in crime surveys.[21] As the introduction to the European Union survey on violence notes, 'women can perpetrate violence, and men and boys can be victims of violence at the hands of both sexes, but the results of this survey, together with other data collection, show that violence against women is predominantly perpetrated by men.'[22]

Violence against women, and against other men, is linked to the way that men are brought up and the perception they are given of what it means to be a man. Lori Heise, senior lecturer at the London School of Hygiene and Tropical Medicine and chief executive of STRIVE, an international research consortium studying the structural drivers of HIV, notes: 'The more I work on violence against women, the more I become convinced that the real way forward is to redefine what it means to be male.'[23]

As it is mainly men who use violence, working with men on violence has to be part of the feminist project. The majority of men do not use violence, but they are part of a patriarchal system where such violence is seen as acceptable, and they may well stand by or fail to intervene when they see violence or hear sexist language and behavior. Shockingly, one of the biggest factors in men using violence is if they have experienced or witnessed violence themselves as a child.[24]

A group of men working against violence in the Dominican Republic discussed the fact that many of them had been beaten by their fathers, or had seen their mothers being beaten. They didn't want to do the same to their own children and were worried about rising levels of violence against women. 'My parents treated us as animals,' a man named Cristobal explained. 'We worked, we never went to school. I wanted to make a different family but didn't know how. So my *compadres* and I have started to meet and exchange ideas. I hope my children will treat their children differently.' Emilio agreed: 'I am a father. I have given confidence to my children, I know that to teach them I must not hit them. Violence in the home can cause delinquency – if a child sees violence they will be violent.'

The men felt that the increase in violence was at least in part due to the fact that women were now educated, often to a higher degree than men, and that many were the main wage-earners, migrating to the cities or even abroad for work. 'When women exercise their rights today,' said Manuel, 'men are not educated about those rights. So when a woman starts to demand her rights, men get angry. Men need to know how to change their way of thinking.' Rudio added: 'If there is women's liberation, it is a shock for men's reality. And that is how the violence gets worse.'[25]

Ringing the Bell: ending men's violence against women

In India, the Bell Bajao ('Ring the Bell') project began in 2008 as a cultural and media campaign that called on men and boys to take a stand against domestic violence by literally ringing the doorbell if they heard violence in a neighbor's home. 'Men and women together have responded with outrage to recent dramatic acts of violence from Delhi to Cairo to Steubenville,' stated the campaign's website. 'We know that effective laws, courts and cops are essential – but they are not enough. We need individual and community action to challenge the habits and norms that perpetuate violence.'

Pramod Tiwari, a government worker, explained what happened to him: 'In front of my house, there is a family that drags the woman by her hair. They drag her near the gas and say "burn yourself". They don't give her food. In winters I see her without warm clothes. In summers she has no fan. She stays locked in a room, like a prisoner. After watching the Bell Bajao ads, we started making some noise every time we heard violence. The violence used to stop for the time being. Eventually it stopped entirely. I want to thank Bell Bajao for inspiring me to take action.'[26]

In Britain, a group of men involved in campaigns for custody of their children express the same sentiments in a different way. They feel that the system is stacked against them, and they blame not only the mother, but all women, especially feminists, for the pain they experience through not being allowed to see their children.

So it is important when men in the public eye, such as US Senator Joe Biden, speak out. 'You guys in the audience,' Biden said at the White House's United State of Women summit in June 2016, 'we've got to overcome this social discomfort of calling out the misogyny that happens when no women are present: the locker-room talk, the bar banter, the rape jokes. As a man, maybe it makes you uncomfortable, but if you let it pass because you want to become one of the other guys, you become an accomplice.'[27]

Projects that encourage men to stand up against

violence are key. And there are many of them. The White Ribbon campaign of men against violence against women, founded in 1991 by a group of pro-feminist men as a response to the killing of female students in a college in Ontario, Canada, has now spread to more than 60 countries.[28] Other campaigns are local or national, or specific to colleges and campuses, where violence and harassment of women has been on the increase.[29]

Silencing women

One of the things that comes across most strongly from accounts of violence against women is that it has the potential to silence us. Women who have been raped or assaulted may feel that it is *their* reputation, rather than their attackers', which is under scrutiny. Women who are brave enough to stand up in court to face their assailant often find themselves in front of (mostly male) judges who question their sexual history or rule that they were wearing 'inappropriate clothing'. In Colombia, a government report found that 37 per cent of respondents believed that 'women who dress provocatively expose themselves to violence'.[30] In South Africa, a survey of 250,000 young people in school found that young men believed 'girls have no right to refuse sex with their boyfriends; girls mean yes when they say no; girls like sexually violent guys; girls who are raped ask for it; girls enjoy being raped'.[31] In Britain, a survey for Amnesty International found that more than one in four respondents thought a woman was 'partially or totally responsible' if she was raped when wearing sexy or revealing clothing. More than one in five held the same view if she had had many sexual partners.[32]

In a blog on the Feminism in India website, a young woman called Swetha expressed her annoyance when a police officer told the boys in the school to leave the room so that she could talk to the girls about not wearing 'provocative' clothing. 'Sorry to break it to you people,' Swetha wrote, 'but this claim wouldn't be valid even in a twisted world where women's clothes are responsible for crimes against them. Sexual harassment is a manifestation of power.'[33]

In the Brock Turner case, the victim wrote about what felt like a second assault – on her reputation: 'After a physical assault, I was assaulted with questions designed to attack me, to say, "See, her facts don't line up, she's out of her mind, she's practically an alcoholic, she probably wanted to hook up, he's like an athlete right, they were both drunk".'

On top of this, she was terrified of being identified. She told Turner in her letter: 'You made my own hometown an uncomfortable place to be.'[34]

Women who do report a rape or assault are often unlikely to find justice, even if there are laws in place to protect them – which in many countries there are not.

- In El Salvador, a law on domestic violence was passed in 2011. In the 16 months after it was passed, only 16 of 63 reported cases were followed up.
- In the state of Rio de Janeiro in Brazil, 1,822 rapes were reported in the first three months of 2013. Only 70 men were arrested.[35]
- In Britain, only 5.7 per cent of reported rape cases result in the perpetrator being convicted.[36]
- Research in 11 countries found that fewer than six per cent of physical and sexual assaults saw charges brought against the perpetrator, and only one to five per cent of cases resulted in convictions. [37]

Research by the United Nations found that in most countries, less than 40 per cent of women who experienced violence sought any kind of help. When they did, it was mostly from family and friends, not the police or health services. Less than 10 per cent turned to the police. As the World's Women 2015 report noted: 'Women's reluctance to seek help may be linked to the widespread acceptability of violence against women.'[38]

Laws that not only make it possible for women to press charges, but also increase awareness of women's rights, are therefore key, as is a judicial system that takes accusations seriously. In Egypt, a new law has criminalized sexual harassment, with immediate results. 'We [have] started to hear about girls going to the police to report sexual harassment in the streets, for instance,' says Yara Fathi Abdel-Salam, who works with the group Appropriate Communication Techniques for Development (ACT). 'This was a result of the modification that took place in this law, and also from raising awareness among girls and women that there is a law now that criminalizes these actions. This would not happen before, that a girl would go to the police to complain about a sexual-harassment incident. But now, step by step, we start to hear about complaints raised to police.'[39]

HarassMap in Egypt

HarassMap has been working against sexual harassment since 2014. The group operates a website where women can report incidents of sexual harassment, which are then mapped online. (Women can also send incident reports through Facebook, Twitter and SMS.) 'When we launched five years ago, it provided a space for women to talk about harassment. This kind of space did not exist before,' says Noora Flinkman. 'It also helps us gather data on this issue – it helps us show that this is actually happening. For a long time there wasn't any evidence of the magnitude of the problem, but now we have data to show it.'

In fact, a 2013 study by UN Women showed that 99.3 per cent of women in Egypt had experienced sexual harassment. 'It is very normalized and socially accepted,' says Noora. 'It affects mobility, sense of safety and security, the ability to perform well, whether it's in your workplace or at school. Not feeling safe restricts women in so many ways, including in political and social life, so it restricts women on an individual level, but it also extends to wider society.'[40]

In 2014, the United Nations published a *Handbook on Effective Prosecution Responses to Violence Against Women and Girls* which sets out guidelines and best practices.[41] These can be the basis for ensuring that women and girls feel safe to report violence, and that they know that justice will be served when they do so.

Online abuse: writing under my real name?

Feminism seems to provoke particular fury online. Perhaps this is because it now has such a public profile; women who stand up or speak out somehow become the focus of men's (and other women's) rage. As British writer Laurie Penny has pointed out, 'the people sending these messages are often perfectly ordinary men holding down perfectly ordinary jobs.' She cites a particularly vile and violent comment that was written by a Richard White, 'who lived in Sidcup, outside London, with a wife and kids, and just happened to run a hate website directed at women and minorities'.[42]

A survey by *The Guardian*[43] of the 70 million online comments left on its site since 2006 found that eight of the ten most abused writers were women, despite the fact that men wrote the greater proportion of articles. Since 2010, those pieces written by women have consistently attracted a higher proportion of blocked comments than those written by men. Articles about feminism attracted very high levels of blocked comments, as have those about rape.

The research also showed a clear link between misogyny and racism and homophobia: of the eight women in the list, four were white and four non-white, and two were gay. The two men in the list were both black and one of them was gay.[44]

Jessica Valenti, who had the dubious honor of being 'top' in the poll, wrote: 'I often wonder, if I could do it over again, would I write under my real name? I certainly could have spared myself and my family a lot of grief if I had written about feminism anonymously.

I wouldn't have had to leave my house in a hurry, my one-year-old daughter in tow, when authorities considered a particular threat credible and dangerous. I would never have listened to abusive voicemails or worried for my safety at public events'.[45]

British freelance writer Eleanor O'Hagan noticed that making feminist arguments led to more abuse:

'As a result, I rarely wrote about feminism at all... To me, misogynistic abuse is an attempt to silence women. Traditionally, men have been the ones who influence the direction of society: I think there is still a sense that it's not women's place to be involved in politics. That's why the abuse women writers experience is really pernicious and needs to stop. Women will never achieve equality so long as they're being intimidated out of the picture.'[46]

Online abuse can easily shift into offline danger – as women from all over the world can testify.[47] Mary Beard, an eminent British historian who faced a barrage of online abuse – and dealt with it by befriending one of her attackers – wrote: 'The misogyny here is truly gobsmacking [and] more than a few steps into sadism. It would be quite enough to put many women off appearing in public, contributing to political debate.'[48] And British comedian Kate Smurthwaite has written: 'What frightens me the most is when an abusive message includes my personal details. I've had my own address quoted at me with a rape threat and – yes – that is terrifying. That's when I call the police; they're not much help.'[49] Jo Cox, the British MP murdered in the street in June 2016, was one of a number of female parliamentarians who also suffered from online abuse.

The abuse is as global as the internet, of course. The Association for Progressive Communications found that online abuse was prevalent in all the countries studied, including Bosnia and Herzegovina, Colombia, Kenya, Mexico, Pakistan, and the Philippines.[50]

Children suffer, too. A survey in Britain by Girlguiding of more than 500 eleven to sixteen-year-old girls found that 45 per cent said they had experienced bullying through social media.[51] The consequences of this for their mental health are alarming – 85 per cent of girls aged 11 to 21 who suffered bullying said it made them feel isolated and lonely, and 69 per cent said that it stopped them speaking out about their views. The same percentage said it made them less interested in their school/college work and 66 per cent said it stopped them going out with their friends. These effects were felt more among the girls who were 17 or older, with just under half saying that the bullying led to their taking more risks than they usually would.

What is particularly frightening is that it doesn't seem to be getting any better. 'Harassers largely go unchecked by social-media companies and media platforms,' explains Jessica Valenti. 'Law enforcement agencies still haven't sorted how to deal with online abusers; and perpetrators are still celebrated as "free speech" warriors. We are a world of smart, innovative people – if there's enough will to change the culture of online commenting, it can be done. But that requires taking the issue seriously, and putting the voices of those most impacted at the forefront of the conversation.'[52]

#ImagineaFeministInternet[53]

In 2014, the Association for Progressive Communications held a meeting of more than 50 feminists in Malaysia. They came up with 15 Feminist Principles of the Internet, beginning with the statement: 'A feminist internet starts with and works towards empowering more women and queer persons – in all our diversities – to dismantle patriarchy. This includes universal, affordable, unfettered, unconditional and equal access to the internet.' The Principles covered access, violence, privacy, pornography and participation.

Conclusion: feminist action for change

A feminist project against violence against women would bring together legislation (ensuring that women at senior levels were involved in drawing it up), changes in attitudes (including media campaigns), support for women who have been subject to violence, and a raft of other measures for protection against violence, including training for those in the system. It would also go wider, to look at gender-based violence as a whole, including the drivers of men's violence against men.

Raghida Ghamlouch, a social worker with the Lebanese Council to Resist Violence Against Women, explains how change begins to happen when these elements come together:

'When I started working on violence against women 11 years ago, it was catastrophic. There was no infrastructure in Lebanon, no talk about [violence against women] in the media. Now it is very different, a 180-degree change. The media is making it a priority to highlight [violence against women]. Before, it was completely missing in the minds of the community, of society as a whole. Talking about this issue was a taboo; now it is not. Now, we have a law [condemning violence against women]; we have several NGOs working on the issue, not just one NGO. For a long time we were the only one. We are now even starting to involve men in our cause, which shows a big difference.'[54]

But perhaps the most important factor in ending violence against women is the one that is the subject of this book: feminism itself. The *American Political Science Review* published the findings of a study on violence against women in 70 countries across four decades. It found that a 'strong autonomous feminist movement is both substantively and statistically significant as a predictor of government action to redress violence against women'.[55] In other words, if we want to end violence against women, we need to redouble feminist action for change, and enlist men to support us in ending this epidemic, once and for all.

1 *Declaration on the Elimination of Violence against Women*, UN General Assembly, 1993. **2** *Report of the Fourth World Conference on Women*, UN, 1995. **3** *The Guardian*, nin.tl/stanford-assault **4** Ibid. **5** UN Women, nin.tl/ending-violence **6** Maha Muna, 'Addressing violence against women through the health system: The case of Kiribati,' UNFPA Pacific Sub-regional Office, 2014; UNFPA and Secretariat of the Pacific Community, Kiribati Family Health and Support Study: A Study on Violence against Women and Children. Both cited in UN Women, *Progress of the World's Women 2015-2016 Transforming Economies, Realizing Rights*, New York 2015. **7** 'The nature, extent, incidence and impact of domestic violence against women in the states of Andhra Pradesh, Chhattis-garh, Gujarat, Madhya Pradesh and Maharashtra', submitted to the Planning Commission, Government of India, New Delhi. **8** UNODC, nin.tl/UNODCtrafficking **9** *How widespread is violence against women?* UN Department of Public Information, 2008. **10** BuzzFeed, nin.tl/stanford-letter **11** *How widespread is violence against women?* op cit. **12** Ibid. **13** Girls' Attitudes Survey 2015, Girlguiding, nin.tl/GGsurvey **14** worldvaluessurvey. org **15** E Fulu et al, 'Why Do Some Men Use Violence against Women and How Can We Prevent It?, Quantitative Findings from the UN Multi-Country Study on Men and Violence in Asia and the Pacific,' Partners for Prevention, 2013. **16** *How widespread is violence against women?* op cit. **17** *El Espectador*, nin.tl/colombia-women **18** E Gracia, 'Intimate Partner Violence against Women and Victim-Blaming Attitudes among Europeans,' WHO Bulletin 92, No 5, 2014. **19** Survey for the Department of Gender issues, Institute for Socio-Economic Studies of Population Russian Academy of Sciences, 2014. **20** World Bank, nin.tl/wb-indicators **21** J L Lauritsen et al, *Trends in the gender gap in violent offending: new evidence from the national crime victimization survey*, Volume 47 Number 2, American Society of Criminology, 2009. **22** Violence against women: an EU-wide survey: main results', European Union Agency for Fundamental rights, 2014. **23** Lori Heise, 'What works to prevent partner violence: an evidence overview', STRIVE Research Consortium, London, 2011. **24** R Levtov, Nikki van der Gaag, M Greene, M Kaufman and G Barker, 'State of the World's Fathers: A MenCare Advocacy Publication', Promundo, Rutgers, Save the Children, Sonke Gender, Justice, and the MenEngage Alliance, Washington DC, 2015. **25** Nikki van der Gaag et al, 'State of the World's Girls 2011: So what about the boys?' Plan International. **26** bellbajao.org/home/about/ **27** Fortune, nin.tl/biden-to-men **28** whiteribboncampaign.co.uk **29** XY Online, nin.tl/xy-men **30** *The Economist*, nin.tl/everyday-agg **31** Alan Greig, Dean Peacock, Rachel Jewkes and Sisonke Msimang, 'Gender and AIDS: time to act', *AIDS 2008*, Lippincott Williams & Wilkins. **32** Amnesty UK, *Sexual Assault Research*, Amnesty, London, 2005. **33** Feminism India, nin.tl/fem-india **34** *The Guardian*, nin.tl/stanford-statement **35** *The Economist*, op cit. **36** Kelly, Lovett and Regan, *A gap or a chasm? Attrition in reported rape cases*, 2005. See also rapecrisis.org.uk/statistics.php

37 H Johnson et al., *Violence Against Women: An International Perspective.* The 11 countries were Australia, Costa Rica, the Czech Republic, Denmark, Greece, Hong Kong, Italy, Mozambique, the Philippines, Poland and Switzerland. **38** United Nations, nin.tl/UN-worlds-women **39** Sisterhood, nin.tl/stemming-tide **40** Sisterhood, op cit. **41** UNODC, 'Handbook on Effective Prosecution,' 2014. **42** *New Statesman,* nin.tl/internet-hate **43** *The Guardian,* nin.tl/dark-side-comments **44** Ibid. **45** *The Guardian,* nin.tl/valenti-threats **46** *New Statesman,* nin.tl/rippedout **47** *The Guardian,* nin.tl/online-abusers **48** *The Telegraph,* nin.tl/beard-on-misogyny **49** *New Statesman,* op cit. **50** genderit.org/onlinevaw/ **51** Girls' Attitudes Survey 2015, op cit. **52** *The Guardian,* nin.tl/online-writers **53** GenderIT, nin.tl/three-key-issues **54** Sisterhood, op cit. **55** M Htun and S L Weldon, 'The civic origins of progressive policy change: combating violence against women in global perspective, 1975-2005', *American Political Science Review* 106.3, 2012.

6 Taking back our bodies: a feminist project

Women's bodies are under scrutiny more than they ever have been. The pressure to conform to media ideals has led to a rise in eating disorders and body shame, and pornography and sex work are hotly debated topics among feminists. We need to reclaim our bodies just as they are and fight against their objectification.

Introduction: our bodies, ourselves?

Much of the focus of those who want to control women's lives is on our bodies. Whether this is the media telling us what shape and size we should be, or pornography that treats our bodies as objects, or religious leaders ordaining how many children we can have or what we can and cannot wear, women's bodies have long been a battleground on which ideological struggles have been fought.

Our Bodies Ourselves: a health book by and for women was a pioneering feminist text from the 1970s, produced by the Boston Women's Collective and subsequently published in many other countries. The idea behind the book was to teach women what doctors did not tell them about their own bodies, as the introduction explained: 'Our bodies are the physical bases from which we move out into the world; ignorance, uncertainty – even, at worst, shame – about our physical selves creates an alienation from ourselves that keeps us from being the whole people that we should be.' It was a deeply political and deeply feminist text, at a time where there was no internet and no other way of learning about our own bodies.

Today, women and girls – at least, those with access to the internet – should be able to find out online all they need to know about the topics covered in that book. Subjects included anatomy and physiology; sexuality; sexual relationships, including lesbian relationships; taking care of ourselves; violence; birth control and abortion; pregnancy, birth and parenthood; and the menopause. But much of the media, including social media, does not necessarily tell you about the feminist approach to women's own bodies as clearly as those pioneering women did in the 1970s.

It could be argued that such an approach is no longer needed. Women's and girls' health has improved hugely:

- Women are living longer than ever before. In Ethiopia, for example, life expectancy for women rose from 50 in 1995 to 65 in 2012.[1]
- Fewer mothers are dying in childbirth. What is known as the maternal mortality rate went down by 40 per cent between 1995 and 2013 in 76 countries and by almost 60 per cent in South Asia.[2]
- The global mortality rate for girls and boys under five fell by 50 and 48 per cent respectively between 1990 and 2013.[3]
- Increasing numbers of women have access to family planning. Use of modern contraception has increased from 53 to 58 per cent worldwide.[4] This has led to the birth rate dropping by more than 20 per cent in 20 years.[5]

However, despite these important gains, there have been setbacks, and there are still areas where improvements are needed. For example, although life expectancy for women has increased in most of the world, in some countries in sub-Saharan Africa it has actually fallen in recent years, due to HIV and AIDS.[6] In Botswana, for example, life expectancy for women fell from 60 in 1995 to 46 in 2012. Worldwide, HIV infection rates have been increasing more quickly for women than for men,[7] with young women aged 15 to 24 now having infection rates twice as high as young men.[8]

About 800 women still die every day from largely preventable causes related to pregnancy and childbirth, mostly in the Global South.[9] Religious authorities still ban contraception, and abortion remains hotly contested in many countries. More than 220 million women in the Global South are still not able to use modern contraception, mostly due to lack of access.[10] And large disparities exist, not only between rich and poor countries, but between wealthier and poorer women within those countries (see Chapter 2).

The need for women and girls to understand how their bodies work, and to campaign for their sexual and reproductive health and rights, is as important now as it was in the 1970s when the Boston feminists first put their book together.

Sexual objectification

In the feminist heyday of the 1960s and 1970s, women used to campaign against advertisements that portrayed women as sexualized beings. Posters of a woman draped across a sports car would have 'My day job is a brain surgeon' graffitied on them in big, bold letters. Today, the images are so ubiquitous that it would be hard to do this.

Sexual objectification, said Caroline Heldman, Associate Professor of Politics at Occidental College in Los Angeles, California, in a TEDx talk in San Diego, is 'the process of treating another person like a sex object, one that serves another's sexual pleasure.'[11] She notes that 96 per cent of sexually objectified bodies are female, and that this way of using women's bodies has become so common that it is the new normal, to the extent that we rarely question it. The consequences for women themselves, she says, are:

- Depression
- Habitual body monitoring (every 30 seconds)
- Eating disorders
- Depressed cognitive functioning

- Sexual dysfunction
- Lower self-esteem
- Lower political efficacy
- Lower school grades
- Female competition
- Body shame.

Sexualized images of women are so common that they have an effect on how girls view themselves. The American Psychological Association's Task Force on the Sexualization of Girls expressed its concern about the negative effects of this sexualized culture, including on girls' cognitive functioning, physical and mental health, sexuality, attitudes and beliefs.[12] The report noted: 'In study after study, findings have indicated that women more often than men are portrayed in a sexual manner (e.g. dressed in revealing clothing, with bodily postures or facial expressions that imply sexual readiness) and are objectified (e.g. used as a decorative object, or as body parts rather than a whole person).

A woman's right to choose

Around a quarter of the world's women live in countries with highly restrictive abortion laws, mostly in Latin America, Africa and Asia, but also in Ireland and Malta. Lack of access to legal and safe abortion can lead to suffering and, sometimes, death. In some countries where abortion is legal, conservative forces are attempting to turn back the clock. In El Salvador, where abortion has been banned since 1988, Congress was considering a proposal to imprison women for up to 50 years for terminating a pregnancy. *The Guardian* notes that 'in some cases, abortions are already treated as murder. Pregnant women who turn up at hospitals bleeding are sometimes handcuffed to the bed. Others are forced to go through births even when their lives are at risk, such as Beatriz, a 22-year-old woman who almost died because she was not permitted to terminate her pregnancy with a fetus that was missing large parts of its brain and skull.'[13] In Ireland, where abortion is illegal, Savita Halappanavar died of septicemia in 2012 after doctors refused to carry out the procedure.[14]

In addition, a narrow (and unrealistic) standard of physical beauty is heavily emphasized. These are the models of femininity presented for young girls to study and emulate.'

It was for this reason that Deborah Tolman and Lyn Mikel Brown felt moved to set up SPARK (Sexualization Protest: Action, Resistance, Knowledge) in the US,[15] which is run by girls and young women. It aims to 'reject the sexualized images of girls in media and support the development of girls' healthy sexuality and self-esteem'.

'I am not for sale': the pressure to look perfect

Tied into the sexualization of women and girls is the fact that they are constantly bombarded with Photoshopped images of models with size zero bodies, which increases the pressure on them to look 'perfect' too.[16] The American National Association of Anorexia Nervosa and Associated Disorders found that about 70 per cent of girls aged 10 to 18 said that 'magazine images influence their ideals of a perfect body.'[17]

'Despite decades of feminist critique of the tyranny of beauty, monitoring and manipulating their appearance remains a daily feature of women's lives,' says UK Feminista founder Kat Banyard. 'Today it is "normal" for women to worry about their looks when they get up each morning, to religiously check their appearance in the mirror throughout the day, to not want to leave the house without make-up on, or to feel fat and disgusted at the sight of their thighs.'[18]

Naomi Wolf wrote in *The Beauty Myth* that 'a culture fixated on female thinness is not an obsession about female beauty, but an obsession about female obedience. Dieting is the most potent political sedative in women's history; a quietly mad population is a tractable one.'[19]

Dieting is not an eating disorder, though it can go on to become one. There are many complex causes for eating disorders such as anorexia nervosa and bulimia, but there seems to be no doubt that they are on the increase, particularly among young women. The National Institute for Health and Care Excellence (NICE) guidelines on eating disorders found that 1.6 million people in Britain were affected by eating disorders in 2004 – of whom 89 per cent were girls and women.[20] In the US, eating disorders affect 10 million women and girls and one million men and boys.[21] The causes of anorexia nervosa, which has the highest mortality rate of any mental illness, are complex.[22] It particularly affects young women, and its consequences are serious: it can cause premature osteoporosis, lack of menstrual periods, exhaustion and even death.[23]

Feminist Celia Edell, in a vlog for *Everyday Feminism*, noted that women internalize the sexist messages that society presents to us. In terms of our looks, 'we are simultaneously told two conflicting messages at once: that looks are incredibly important, and we should do and buy everything in our power to avoid ageing, avoid any imperfections, and to achieve an impossible ideal in order to be successful or even just lovable; and that focusing on your looks is superficial and vain, and that

Sparking change

Fourteen-year-old SPARK member Julia Bluhm's petition urging *Seventeen* magazine to change its policy of using Photoshop to 'improve' how its models look led to a protest outside the offices – and more than 80,000 signatures from around the world.

'We should focus on people's personalities, not just how they look,' Julia told a radio interviewer. 'If you're looking for a girlfriend who looks like the models that you see in magazines, you're never going to find one, because those people are edited with computers.'[24]

Julia was invited to a meeting with *Seventeen*'s editor-in-chief, Ann Shoket, who then announced that the faces and body sizes of the models in its magazine would not be digitally altered. 'This is a huge victory, and I'm so unbelievably happy,' said Julia.[25]

there's something wrong with that. Women are meant to be unbelievably pretty, but not meant to care about their looks too much, either.'[26]

This has international implications. Such beliefs have led to a rise in cosmetic surgery in many parts of the world. In some countries, as such interventions become cheaper and easier, they become increasingly common.

- Brazil leads the world in cosmetic surgery. It has less than three per cent of the world's population, but accounted for 12.9 per cent of cosmetic operations in 2013. This included 515,776 breasts reshaped, 380,155 faces tweaked, 129,601 tummies tucked, 13,683 vaginas reconstructed, 219 penises enlarged and 63,925 buttocks augmented.[27] Plastic surgery is tax deductible.
- One in five South Korean women has had cosmetic surgery.[28]
- Iran, where women cover their hair and bodies but not their noses, leads the world in rhinoplasty.[29]
- In the US, there were 15 million cosmetic procedures in 2014, with the numbers increasing year on year.[30]
- In India, there is a huge market in whitening creams, which now even extend to vaginal whitening.[31]

So why do women and girls (and some men and boys) struggle so much with their self-image? Part of the answer can once again be found not only in the internet and the exponential rise in the number of images we see every day, but in the way that the neoliberal project has privileged the individual over the collective, positing 'choice' and individual empowerment as the answer.

In doing so, however, it has forgotten the fundamental question: in what context are these choices being made? Will being thin or having bigger breasts improve my life? Research seems to show that these endless quests for bodily perfection are in fact as fruitless as any other quests for an unreachable ideal.

As journalist Karen Kay wrote in a piece in the *Observer* entitled 'Is cosmetic surgery the new acceptable face of womanhood?': 'That quick "fix" offers a euphoric high that soon wears off and sees them coming back for more. I believe that cosmetic intervention is addictive and, because we gradually lose sight of the person who once looked back at us in the mirror, all perspective starts to go.' The link with mental health is clear.

Feminists need to see the complexity of such issues. Condemning other women for their choices is not helpful. We need to find ways of tackling the objectification and self-esteem issues that afflict young women in particular, who are, in any case, leading the way in these debates.

We also need to put the many reasons why we struggle with our body image firmly back in the context of the patriarchal society, as feminist writer Julie Doubleday points out:

'Feminism is a fight for equality and, as we're so fond of saying, it's not men versus women. It's misogynists versus those who work to dismantle misogyny. I want to work to dismantle the system that invites me to focus on my appearance before I focus on my world. I want to work to dismantle the system that tells me I will be happier with bigger breasts and smaller thighs. I want to work to dismantle the system that encourages me to see myself as an object with a price tag, whether that feels good or not. I am not for sale. I am not a [size] 1 or a 5 or a 10. I am a person, and a feminist. I am working to understand this strange, exhausting world, and I will work to change it.'[32]

Beyond the margins: sex workers or prostitutes?

Often one of the most marginalized groups in any society are those who sell sex, the majority of whom are women. For feminists, this is a hugely contested area, particularly in relation to whether selling sex is work or violence against women, and there are committed feminists who are equally passionate in their convictions on both sides of the argument.

Those who argue for sex workers' rights feel strongly that only decriminalization will encourage safe working conditions and access to effective HIV and health services. There are now many organizations of sex-worker activists all over the world. The Global Network of Sex Work Projects (NSWP) exists 'to uphold the voice of sex workers globally and connect regional networks advocating for the rights of female, male and transgender sex workers. It advocates for rights-based health and social services, freedom from abuse and discrimination, and self-determination for sex workers.'[33]

Among feminist organizations that support this approach is the Association for Women in Development (AWID), which notes: 'Our starting point... should be that "sex work is work" and our strategic aim... should be to join with women to coalition build and strategize about ways of working within our movements to advance the rights of all women and all workers.'[34]

On the other side are those who argue that prostitution is not only a violation of women's rights, but also violence against women. Engaging with sex work 'first and foremost as a labor issue,' argues Kat Banyard, 'using the term "sex work" as if it was an adequate and appropriate shorthand for what takes place in strip clubs, on porn sets and in brothels, serves a deeply political goal. Not only does this framework shrink the field of analysis to the seller (to the exclusion of men's demand and its social impact), it hides what should be front and center of our response to the transaction: the inherent sexual abuse.'[35]

Both sides would agree that there are some clear areas where sex work/prostitution is violence against women – when it involves children, or trafficking, for example. But sometimes these lines are less obvious.

Meena Saraswathi Seshu and Aarthi Pai, from India, argue[36] that the binary division between sex work as work and prostitution as exploitation 'fails to recognize the dynamics of an institution that encompasses a wide spectrum of elements, from violence and exploitation at one end to autonomy and agency to choose the best possible options at the other.' They go on to outline a fascinating dialogue that took place between sex workers and married women, with each group talking about the ways that a patriarchal society serves to control women through sex. In the end, it was the married women who felt they had less control over their lives and their bodies.

Gary Barker, from Instituto Promundo, an NGO that works in violence prevention and gender equality, also argues that neither side is asking the right question, which should be: why are men buying sex in the first place? He cites research in Latin America, Asia and sub-Saharan Africa which finds that 'men who admit they have paid for sex are more likely to hold negative views or misogynistic attitudes about women, and are more likely to have reported carrying out rape than men who say they have never paid for sex with a sex worker.' His solution? To 'create spaces to talk about desire, sex, bodies and pleasure in ways that are respectful and not degrading. Maybe then we could move toward reducing some of the demand for sex work before it starts.'[37]

Seshu and Pai's paper notes that 'feminists and sex workers have only recently begun to talk to each other. New learning needs to occur within feminist theory to include the experiences of these women who stand beyond the margins and have a different story to narrate.' At the moment, it seems difficult to find the spaces for this kind of dialogue to happen.

Pornography: oppression or empowerment?

Feminism has often taken different sides when it comes to pornography too. There are those like US radical feminists Catherine McKinnon and the late Andrea Dworkin, who are clearly anti-porn and see it as violence against women. In her 1981 book, *Pornography: Men Possessing Women*, Dworkin wrote: 'Pornography is a celebration of rape and injury to women; it's a kind of union for rapists, a way of legitimizing rape and formalizing male supremacy in our society.'[38]

Then there are liberal feminists who say that they are not necessarily for or against but that they are in favor of freedom of speech, and that therefore porn should be allowed.

More recently, there has been a movement for 'feminist porn' with the launch of the Feminist Porn Awards in 2006.[39] The website of the Feminist Porn Awards gives a definition of the term:[40]

- Actors are treated with respect, paid fairly, given choice and ethical working conditions, empowered in their work.
- Directors collaborate with and incorporate the actor's own sexual desires and fantasies (makes for better scenes too!).
- It expands the boundaries of sexual representation on film and challenges stereotypes, especially of women and marginalized communities.
- Realistic pleasure is depicted.

Whatever one thinks of feminist porn, it goes against the mainstream. With violent and degrading images so readily available on the internet, the overarching theme of much pornography is deeply misogynistic. For example, a content analysis in the US of 50 best-selling adult videos found that:[41]

- Nearly half of the 304 scenes analysed contained verbal aggression.
- Over 88 per cent showed physical aggression.

- 72 per cent of aggressive acts were perpetrated by men.
- 94 per cent of these acts were committed against women.
- Fewer than five per cent of the aggressive acts provoked a negative response from the victim, such as flinching and requests to stop.

More positive behaviors, such as verbal compliments, embracing, kissing or laughter, were largely absent.[42]

Does this affect relationships in real life? According to a study in Australia by masculinities expert Michael Flood: 'There is compelling evidence from around the world that pornography has negative effects on individuals and communities... porn is a very poor sex educator because it shows sex in unrealistic ways and fails to address intimacy, love, connection or romance. Often it is quite callous and hostile in its depictions of women.'[43]

Another study found that 'youth who look at violent X-rated material are six times more likely to report forcing someone to do something sexual online or in person versus youth not exposed to X-rated material.'[44]

US feminist Jessica Valenti notes that 'internet porn and the normalization of pornography have spawned a whole new generation of guys who were raised thinking that porn sex equals normal sex. Not to mention a whole generation of girls who think porn sex is the only way to please guys.'[45]

One very obvious link is the trend for complete removal of body hair, including pubic hair. While some feminists may complain that attention should not be focused on something so trivial, making your vagina look like a child's or a porn star's has clear political connotations. In a survey of 3,316 women in the US, 59 per cent said they had removed their pubic hair for 'hygiene reasons'. Eight-four per cent had removed some hair and 62 per cent said they had removed all their pubic hair at least once. This was most common between the ages of 18 and 24.[46]

Luisa Dillner, a British doctor who writes an advice column, cited the study and pointed out that removing pubic hair, far from being hygienic, actually 'leaves your pubis wounded and defenseless.' She quotes another US study which 'found that the number of emergency department visits for grooming increased fivefold between 2002 and 2010.'[47]

In mid-2016 a spate of articles appeared about a feminist fightback on body hair, from an Instagram discussion about photos of young women showing pubic hair,[48] to 16-year-old Adele Labo's hashtag #LesPrincessesOntDesPoils (Princesses have hair), which became a top trending topic on Twitter,[49] and 22-year-old Indian blogger Naina Kataria's poem and photo about body hair which was shared on Facebook more than 11,000 times.[50]

To return to the pornography debate, Pandora Blake, who makes feminist porn, argues: 'If you dismiss all porn as inherently degrading, you are dismissing the work done by the amazing feminist porn activists and revolutionaries who are working to make porn that empowers participants and viewers alike – porn that challenges gender expectations and subverts stereotypes. Feminist pornographers know that misogynistic male-gaze porn does not serve us as a society. Rather than complaining about it, we are putting our energies to creating something better.'

She continues: 'If you truly care about empowering porn performers, start by reducing poverty. Fight to improve our welfare state, for a citizen's basic income, for more flexible working options for parents and people with disabilities, and for decreased tuition fees for students. It is possible to work full time in this country without earning a living wage, while others who want to work full time may not be able to. If you want to make someone more empowered, you need to give them better options, not fewer options.[51]

Conclusion: reclaiming our bodies for ourselves

Controlling women's bodies is part of the way that a patriarchal society exerts its authority. Fighting back against that control, and freeing women from the internalized misogyny that leads us to obsess about whether our bodies conform to some non-existent ideal, has to be part of the feminist project. But we must also take care not to condemn women who struggle with a whole range of issues around body image.

Dialogue and debate, opening up discussion, and informing ourselves about how our bodies work, were at the heart of the Boston Women's Collective book *Our Bodies Ourselves*. Angela Phillips and Jill Rakusen, writing about putting together the British edition, said: 'Probably the most valuable thing we learned was to speak for ourselves and be ourselves... Gradually, with others' support, we began to rediscover ourselves.' Perhaps there needs to be a new feminist body project for the 21st century. We may not approve of pornography or sex work, but in coming to terms with how women's bodies are marketized and objectified, we also need to recognize each other's views, and put what women themselves want at the heart of the project to reclaim our bodies.

This includes the joy of having a body and the pleasure of sex. As Hannah Wallace Bowman from the NGO Love Matters writes:

'Let's talk about human beings as they are, as a whole, in all their living, breathing, sweaty sexiness. Not as harbingers of disease or reproductive mechanisms, but as people. For the result of a woman understanding her pleasure, owning that pleasure, seeking that pleasure is extremely powerful. It changes the relationship we have with our bodies and the decisions we make about what to do with them.'[52]

1 World Bank, nin.tl/WB-life **2** 'Trends in Maternal Mortality: 1990 to 2013,' WHO, 2014. **3** World Bank, based on estimates developed by the UN Inter-agency Group for Child Mortality Estimation, childmortality. org **4** United Nations Population Division, Estimates and Projections of Family Planning Indicators 2014 **5** World Bank, nin.tl/WB-indicators **6** Global Health Observatory, WHO, nin.tl/WHO-lifeexpectancy **7** UNAIDS nin.tl/UNAIDS-spectrum **8** UNAIDS World Aids Day Report 2011. **9** WHO maternal mortality report 2014. **10** WHO Fact Sheet: 'Family Planning', 2013. **11** YouTube, nin.tl/heldman-tedx **12** 'Report of the APA Task Force on the Sexualization of Girls', American Psychological Association Washington DC, 2007. **13** *The Guardian*, nin.tl/el-salvador-law **14** BBC, nin.tl/abortion-request **15** sparksummit.com **16** Beauty Redefined, nin.tl/redefined-blog **17** *Huffington Post*, nin.tl/eating-disorders-fashion **18** Kat Banyard, *The Equality Illusion*: *The Truth about Women and Men Today*, Faber and Faber, 2010. **19** Naomi Wolf, The *Beauty Myth, How Images of Beauty Are Used Against Women*, Chatto and Windus, 1990. **20** mengetedstoo.co.uk/information/the facts **21** Eating Disorder Hope, nin.tl/eatingdisorders-stats **22** Eating Disorder Hope, nin.tl/mortalitystats **23** Eating Disorder Hope, nin.tl/eatingdisorders-stats **24** Wbur, nin.tl/airbrushing-fashion **25** Spark Movement, nin.tl/17-commits and NPR, nin.tl/photoshop-pledge **26** Everyday Feminism, nin.tl/internalized-misogyny **27** *The Guardian,* nin.tl/nip-and-tuck **28** *Time,* nin.tl/surgery-rise **29** Ibid. **30** *The Guardian*, nin.tl/face-of-womanhood **31** New Internationalist blog, nin.tl/whitening-craze **32** *The Guardian*, nin.tl/low-body-con **33** nswp.org **34** PLRI, nin.tl/awid-istanbul **35** Kat Banyard, *'Pimp State: Sex, Money and the Future of Equality'*, Faber and Faber, 2016, quoted in *The Guardian*, nin.tl/banyard-guardian **36** IDS Bulletin, nin.tl/undressing-patriarchy **37** Promundo, nin.tl/changingdebate **38** *The Guardian,* nin.tl/dworkin-book **39** feministpornawards.com **40** Feminist Porn Awards, nin.tl/fem-porn **41** A Bridges, R Wosnitzer, E Scharrer, C Sun and R Liberman, 'Aggression and sexual behavior in best-selling pornography: a content analysis update', Violence Against Women. **42** R J Wosnitzer and A Bridges, 'Aggression and sexual behavior in best-selling pornography: a content analysis update', paper presented at the 57th Annual Meeting of the International Communication Association, San Francisco, CA, 2007. **43** Michael Flood, 'Harms of pornography exposure among children and young people', *Child Abuse Review*, 18(6), November/December 2009. **44** Center for Disease & Control, *Internet Solutions for Kids*, November 2010 **45** *Feminism: A Young woman's guide to why feminism matters*, Seal Press, 2007. **46** Tami S Rowen, Thomas W Gaither, Mohannad A Awad, E Charles Osterberg, Alan W Shindel, Benjamin N Breyer, 'Pubic Hair Grooming Prevalence and Motivation Among Women in the United States', *JAMA Dermatol*, 2016. **47** *The Guardian*, nin.tl/pubic-hair-debate **48** Style Mic, nin.tl/talking-pubic-hair **49** Dazed, nin.tl/bodyhairstigma **50** Style Mic, nin.tl/bodyhairpoem **51** *New Statesman,* nin.tl/dont-ask-if-porn **52** Awid, nin.tl/awid-repro-health

7 Growing up a feminist: changing attitudes

Even where laws are in place to protect and support women's rights, they are not always implemented. Customs, gender stereotypes and social pressures can hinder progress. But feminists around the world have a vision for a fairer future and, together, we can make it come true.

Introduction: taking care of somebody else's garden

'If we're going to change our policies and our politics, we have to change something else: we have to change the way we see ourselves. We're still boxed in by stereotypes about how men and women should behave. We need to keep changing the attitude that raises our girls to be demure and our boys to be assertive, to criticize our daughters for speaking out and our sons for shedding a tear. We need to change the attitude that punishes women for their sexuality but gives men a pat on the back for theirs.'

Former US President Barack Obama[1]

Changing attitudes and behaviors is perhaps one of feminism's hardest tasks. One of feminism's biggest triumphs has been that laws and policies now exist in many countries that ought to ensure women are equal to men. However, this is often not matched by the reality in practice.

The age-old idea that women and girls are not only different but somehow inferior to men begins even before a baby is born. In Vietnam, a proverb[2] says: 'One son is children, two daughters are none', and in Nepal: 'To raise and care for a daughter is like taking care of somebody else's garden.'[3] In Uganda, a focus group explained that 'if you give birth to a girl she is called *eitawo* [a source of income in the form of dowry or sugar]; a boy is referred to as *emundhu* [gun] or *ozzaire ekirowa* [landmark].[4]

Sex-selective abortion and the infanticide of baby girls because sons are preferred have left at least 117 million girls missing from the world's population.[5] In India, although it is illegal, scanning technology has made it even more possible to abort a fetus on the basis of its sex alone. A study by Action Aid and the International Development Research Centre found that in the more prosperous areas of some northern states of India, the ratio of girls to boys under the age of six is now lower than it was in 2001.[6]

One woman from Haryana explained why she had an abortion when she found out her second fetus was female: 'When I got pregnant the second time, I told my

---

Campaigning against sex-selective abortion

'Here in India, women are blamed for all that is wrong in society,' says Asha Singh, a women's rights campaigner with Prayatn, an organization dedicated to reversing the trend of India's disappearing daughters in Morena.

'Men feel they can inflict pain, shame and dishonor on women because we are powerless to fight back. I am determined to try and change this. I'm a trained lawyer but have been working as an activist fighting against sex discrimination for five years. Every month I travel by motorbike to over 25 towns and villages, talking to women about their rights and asking them to recognize the valuable place they hold in our society. I want to help reduce discrimination against women and stop the violence against girls happening at every level of our society.

'India's disappearing daughters are a national shame. Sex-selective abortions are wrong and it's very difficult to witness parents determining that their baby is worthless because she is a girl. It's also hard to witness how much neglect there is of girls in some of the villages I work in. I want to empower more and more women to come forward, and with their help I can reach more villages and towns. Change doesn't come easily but I am convinced we can change things for the better in India. I'm proud I've become a role model for many girls in rural areas.'[7]

Growing up a feminist

husband, "This society does not value girls and I do not want to give birth to another one". When I gave birth to my first daughter everyone pitied me. The taunts that I would have faced from society and from my in-laws for not having a son forced me to abort. Knowing the amount of harassment my baby would go through after her birth, I think it is much better to die.'[8]

Being a girl, being a boy

Notions of gender are both shaped and internalized in the very early years of a child's life. 'Infant brains are so malleable, says neuroscientist Lise Eliot, 'that small differences at birth become amplified over time, as parents, teachers, peers and the culture at large unwittingly reinforce gender stereotypes.'[9]

A UN report noted that by the age of five 'most girls and boys have already internalized the gender-role expectations communicated to them by their families,

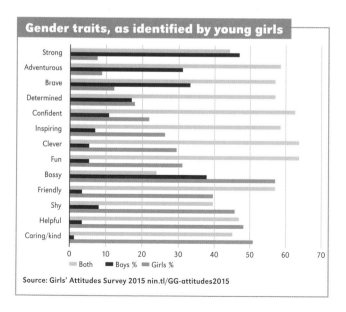

Gender traits, as identified by young girls

Source: Girls' Attitudes Survey 2015 nin.tl/GG-attitudes2015

schools, the media and society... These norms will influence their behavior and their development for the rest of their lives.'[10]

Among young children, ideas about being a boy or a girl are still stereotyped and surprisingly similar around the world. In Britain, research with girls in 2015 by Girlguiding[11] found that 'girls aged 7 to 10 clearly identify some character traits as belonging more to boys than girls – and vice versa. The majority of girls associate the words strong, brave and adventurous with boys more than with girls. The character traits most associated with girls, and least with boys, are caring, helpful and shy.'

These beliefs and attitudes have clear implications for children's behavior and the way that they are treated by adults. Lise Eliot warns: 'Girls are not naturally more empathic than boys, they are just allowed to express their feelings more... Boys are empathetic and can learn to be even more so if we don't exaggerate stereotypes and try to focus on their emotional development as much as their athletic and academic skills.'[12]

The Women's Commission for Refugee Women and Children notes: 'Young boys... are generally allowed more freedoms and have fewer restrictions placed on them than young girls. They are taught to play rough, to stand up for themselves, not to walk away from a fight. They run out to play while their sisters are kept indoors to care for younger children and to help with domestic chores.'[13]

These stereotypes start early and are reinforced throughout a child's early life. Recent initiatives in Sweden and the US for gender-neutral nurseries and kindergartens are a welcome initiative, encouraging children to engage with a wider range of toys and discouraging gender-specific language. At a similar initiative in El Salvador, boys can be found playing at cooking and girls at being firefighters. Alexia, a teacher in the school, says that they also work with parents, who 'see that the boys talk to the girls with more respect and that both boys and girls can share toys and spaces and play together.'[14]

This is important, because early stereotyped behavior not only has consequences for girls, but also means that boys may be discouraged from learning how to help in the home. Focus groups conducted by the World Bank[15] in 20 countries found that one of the most common characteristics of a 'good girl' as seen by both girls and boys is that 'she helps around the house and is well-behaved, obedient and respectful. A good girl also goes to school.' Interestingly, girls think a good boy should also help around the house but 'boys tend to think this is less important than being respectful or doing other things'.

In research in Rwanda, boys aged 12 to 14 said that 'the majority of men fear to do home activities because

Big boys should cry

'Big boys don't cry' is the message often given even to very young boys: don't show or talk about your emotions. But researcher Niobe Way spoke to hundreds of boys in the US and found that in early adolescence, they did share their deepest feelings with their male friends. Around the age of 15, however, they started to shut down – with serious consequences for their mental health.[16]

Jackson Katz, a masculinities expert in the US, notes that boys learn very early that 'being a so-called "real man" means you... have to show the world only certain parts of yourself that the dominant culture has defined as manly.' He goes on to cite a list of what young men themselves define as being a 'real man', including being physical, strong, independent, intimidating, powerful, in control, respected, tough, athletic and a stud. He points out that the worst insult for any boy is to call him a girl.[17]

Psychologist Joseph Pleck from the University of Illinois found that young men who believed in what they saw as traditional masculinity tended to see men and women in opposition to each other. They also had more sexual partners, fewer intimate relationships with their female partners and made less consistent use of condoms.[18]

they think they will be laughed at'.[19] In many countries, daughters have less value than sons.[20] 'If I was in charge,' says 16-year-old Shoeshoe from Lesotho, 'I would get rid of the stereotype of women having to stay at home, doing the cooking and cleaning, taking care of the kids and not going out to work. I would get everybody to see that... women can do anything and men can do anything, and it won't be seen as improper or disrespectful or wrong.'[21]

And in Brazil, Lana, also 16, voices her dream like this: 'If I were president, I would enact a law for equal rights, saying that women and men could do the same things. If she cleans the house, he can do it too; and if she can cook, he can do it too!'[22]

Selling children a lie

One of the ways in which binary views are continually being reinforced is through the kinds of toys that are marketed to children and their parents. It also clearly reveals how consumerism shapes notions of gender. The market for children's toys, books and clothes is worth billions of dollars[23] and in the past 10 years has become increasingly gender-specific, with anything active and blue being for boys, and anything passive and pink for girls. (Interestingly, 100 years ago the *Ladies Home Journal* in the US considered blue to be a color for girls because it was 'delicate and dainty' and pink to be for boys because it was strong.)

'There has been a wholesale "pinkification" of girls,' says Abi Moore, a 38-year-old freelance television producer. 'It's everywhere; you can't escape it. And it needs to change. It sells children a lie – that there's only one way to be a "proper girl" – and it sets them on a journey, at a very, very early age. It's a signpost, telling them that beauty is more valued than brains; it limits horizons, and it restricts ambitions.' Moore and her twin sister Emma co-founded a British campaign called Pink Stinks in 2009 to try to root out the gender and color divide in children's toys, clothing and books.[24]

Their website notes: 'We would like retailers and media to start taking corporate responsibility for the misrepresentation and narrow definitions of girls/women, and ask people to consider the repercussions that we see as strongly linking to pink culture. Cultural change is key. As pink-branding starts from birth, so do these sexist, damaging notions.'

They have had a number of successes. There are now 'Pinkstinks Approved' companies providing non-gender-specific play and learning products for children. Companies such as John Lewis, Marks and Spencer and Sainsbury's have removed the 'girls' label from a pink Playmobil set and a 'boys' label from a science kit[25] and added non-gender-specific labels to children's nurse and doctor outfits.[26] There is now a Pink Stinks campaign in Germany.[27]

Let Toys be Toys[28] is a parent-led campaign in Britain. 'From inflatable pink orcas and Boutique monopoly to pink superman costumes and pink glue (we kid you not!), the idea of taking a regular product, giving it a pink makeover and selling it back to girls is so common that one wonders how girls will cope when they grow up and find out that the world is *not* covered in pastel pink,' notes the campaign, which has launched a good practice award.[29]

The results of its 2013 pre-Christmas survey showed a 60-per-cent reduction in the use of 'girls' and 'boys' signs in stores compared to the previous year. In 2014, its review of online shopping sites selling toys and children's books found a 46-per-cent reduction in the use of gender categorization over two years. In 2015 it carried out research into how girls and boys were represented in TV advertisements for toys and discovered that 'a majority showed boys and girls playing separately in stereotypical ways' but that 'boys and girls were represented in broadly similar numbers, and just under a third of ads showed girls and boys playing together.'[30]

The research shows that there is still a long way to go. Ed Mayo, co-author of *Consumer Kids: How Big Business Is Grooming Our Children for Profit*, argues that the children's market has now reached the stage where 'it's no exaggeration to talk of a gender apartheid'.[31]

But the issue is receiving increasing attention. In April 2016, the White House organized a conference devoted to breaking down gender stereotypes in children's media and toys.[32] Sophie, aged nine, sums it up on the Pink Stinks website:

'Girls like me shouldn't be forced to like pink. Can you think of a good name for girls who don't want to be girly girls but aren't tomboys? My mum and I have been trying to think of one for ages. PINK STINKS!!'[33]

Mental health is a feminist issue

In a 2015 Girlguiding survey in Britain, 58 per cent of respondents aged 13 to 17 cited mental-health issues as their top concern. A majority wanted to know more about where to get help and support and felt that mental-health issues were difficult to talk about. Of those aged 11 to 21, 62 per cent said that they knew a girl or young woman who had experienced a mental-health problem. Two in five of the respondents said they had needed help with their mental health; among those aged 17 to 21 it was nearly half.[34]

A World Health Organization (WHO) study of 220,000 young people in Europe and North America in 2013/14 found that girls reported poorer mental health than boys.[35] These high levels of concern about mental health in women are consistent with other findings all over the world: depression and anxiety are more common in women, and alcoholism and antisocial personality disorders are more common in men. Schizophrenia and bipolar disorder occur at similar rates in both sexes.[36] And while more women attempt suicide, more men succeed, making suicide the most common killer of young men in many countries.[37]

The WHO notes: 'Gender is a critical determinant of mental health and mental illness... [and] determines the differential power and control men and women have over the socio-economic determinants of their mental health and lives, their social position, status and treatment in society and their susceptibility and exposure to specific mental-health risks.'[38] It also notes that 'pressures created by their multiple roles, gender discrimination and associated factors of poverty, hunger, malnutrition, overwork, domestic violence and sexual abuse, combine to account for women's poor mental health.'

Four reasons why mental health is a feminist issue[40]

I became a feminist because of my mental health. Even before I was comfortable with the words 'eating disorder' to describe what I was experiencing, I grew to love feminist activism because I was comforted by the idea that my body belonged to me, and me alone.

Knowing I had feminism on my side was a major aspect of my ongoing recovery. Feminism taught me self-love and bodily autonomy. More importantly, it was through feminist social media that I was introduced to amazing feminist activists who struggled with the same illnesses I did. I learned I wasn't alone, and that my struggles didn't make me a bad person.

Through feminism, I also grew comfortable calling people out, telling my story, and taking self-care days. But more than my own personal path to feminism via mental health, let's address the ways in which mental health is, at its core, a feminist issue.

1. **Our ideas of gender roles, race, sexuality and class strongly inform and perpetuate how we understand mental health.** Essentially, this means capitalist, white, hetero-patriarchal norms dictate the ways in which people are diagnosed, and therefore treated. This also means access differs depending on these intersecting aspects of identity.

2. **Recovery often requires self-love.** Audre Lorde said it best when she stated: 'Caring for myself is not an act of self-indulgence. It is self-preservation, and that is an act of political warfare.' People with marginalized identities are taught not to

If mental health is still not recognized equally with physical health in the Global North, this is even more true in the Global South, where up to 20 per cent of those attending primary healthcare may suffer from anxiety and/or depressive disorders which are not recognized and therefore not treated. 'When women dare to disclose their problems, many health workers tend to have gender biases which lead them to either over-treat or under-treat women,' according to the WHO.[39]

Once again, the wider issues around gender differences and the power that women and men wield or do not wield over their own lives have a specific impact on mental health. Yet this is a subject that is still not talked about enough, even in feminist circles.

---

love themselves. Feminism stands firmly against that notion and teaches lessons of how to care for oneself. Self-love is revolution.

3. **Because the brain is an organ, and a very important one, caring for mental health is a form of bodily autonomy.** Whether we are discussing body image or an individual's decision to take medication, mental-health activism is largely centered on the idea that we should all be able to make informed decisions about what to do with our health.

4. **We likely would not have feminist activism without a certain extent of mental-health activism.** We know the statistics on mental health: one in four adults live with a diagnosable mental-health disorder. If we apply that statistic to the breadth of the feminist movement, it accounts for a lot of activists. We need to care about mental health because it affects us all.

I am a feminist. I am also someone who experiences mental illness. While these are two intersecting aspects of my life and activism, they are often separated. Let's work harder to incorporate mental health into our activism, not only in theory, but also in practice. This means being aware of people who are unable to be 'activists' in the traditional sense, encouraging self-love and self-care, and actively eliminating ableist language from daily speech. Mental health is a feminist issue because we, as feminist activists, will need to care about our holistic well-being if we are to succeed as a movement.

Laura Jensen, for Feminist Campus

Growing up a feminist

Supporting women's autonomy and self-belief is part of the bedrock of feminism, as Laura Jensen explains (see page 126).

Feminism, FGM and early marriage

There are many practices around the world that exist because of women's subordinate position in the world and the need that society feels to control their bodies and sexuality. But eradicating them is not simple, particularly in situations where families have few material resources to support themselves.

In many countries of the Global South, female genital mutilation (FGM), or female genital cutting as it is also known, has been practiced for hundreds of years. It involves cutting off the clitoris; in the more extreme case of infibulation, the outer labia is removed and the vagina stitched together. The belief is that this keeps a woman chaste and is more satisfying for her husband, but it can lead to infection, and even death, and is often the cause of lifelong pain and complications during sex and birth.

FGM is thought to have affected an estimated 140 million girls and women around the world. In Africa, at least three million girls a year undergo it.[41]

In recent years, campaigns against FGM have led to its being outlawed in an increasing number of countries. The United Nations has declared that FGM is a violation of girls' and women's rights and, more recently, named it as child abuse.[42]

But the issue is complex. It is older women who often carry out the procedure, supported by women in the family who believe that their daughters will never find a husband unless they are 'cut'. When the practice is outlawed, young women have been known to secretly get themselves cut for the same reason.[43]

There has been a troubled relationship between feminists in the West, who started to campaign against the practice in the 1980s, and women within the countries of the Global South where it is practiced who, even if they themselves are against the practice, have felt resentful of what they see as another form of colonialism by white Western women.[44] They believe that eradicating such practices needs to be a combination of legislation and patience while establishing alternative rites of passage.

Tostan, a non-governmental organization that began in Senegal and now works in Djibouti, The Gambia, Guinea, Guinea-Bissau, Mali, Mauritania, Senegal and Somalia, has taken a local approach that allows community members to learn about their rights and the consequences of the practice and to 'draw their own conclusions about FGM and lead their own movements for change'. This non-blame approach has

---

Early marriage in Pakistan

The girl sitting opposite me looks like a child, and at first I assume she is the daughter of one of the women gathered to meet me. It turns out that Hajra is the mother of the baby she is rocking, and that she had another baby who died. Marriage at 15 or earlier is common in Pakistan. Girls are often married once they have their first period, which marks their very abrupt passage from childhood into adulthood.

Most girls who are married this young come from poor families, with many children. They may be married off so that there is one less mouth to feed, or because parents feel that her husband and his family will be better able to look after her. Once a girl is married, family honor, a very important principle in Pakistan, is preserved.

There is conflicting legislation in Pakistan about marriage under the age of 18. In a number of statutes, such as the Child Marriage Restraint Act 1929 (CMRA), a child is defined as 'a person who, if a male, is under 18 years of age, and if a female, is under 16 years of age'. The Hudood Ordinance criminalizes the act of sexual intercourse between adult men and women who are not 'validly married' and notes that an adult is 'a person who has attained, being a male, the age of 18 years or, being a female, the age of 16 years', but crucially adds: 'or has attained puberty'. So there are contradictions in the law which make it hard to prosecute, despite the fact that Pakistan has also signed up to international legislation which prohibits child marriage.

---

helped build a critical mass of support and has led to the abandonment of the practice in 7,200 communities, often through the establishment of alternative non-harmful practices.[45]

Early marriage too, has been the subject of global campaigns. Girls who are married young not only often leave school, but have babies when they are still children, with sometimes horrific physical and mental-health consequences.[46]

Campaigns, feminist or otherwise, need to be carried out with care, recognizing that poor parents may arrange for their daughters to be married when still young because they see this as giving them a better chance in life, or simply of having one less mouth to feed. Until we tackle the poverty that lies at the heart of such choices, early marriage will never be eradicated (see Chapter 2).[47]

Conclusion: changing the future

Changing attitudes and behaviors towards women and girls is going to take a long time. But in many areas of our lives, change has begun. We need to work with women and girls and men and boys to ensure that this continues and to guard against the forces that would seek to move things backwards. The younger generation, who in many countries are more educated than their parents and have access to a wider world through technology, are clear that they want this change to happen:

- 'There is still a stereotype that boys should lead. But this pushed me to perform more and better so I could be the leader – even though I was a girl.'

  Nurul, 17, Indonesia[48]

- 'I have an ambition that my group will be strengthened to reach each and every girl of the community, where no women will be humiliated and have to lead a life like my mother, where no girl will get married early and be tortured by her in-laws, where no girl will drop out from school. All girls will be adored like our brothers.'

Tanuja, young woman in India[49]

- 'We used to be silent at home and not say what we thought. We will not be silent any more.'

Manal, 15, Egypt[50]

- 'Don't put girls and women down and make them feel as if they are inferior to males. Empower them and let them know they can do whatever they want. The past cannot be changed, but the future can.'

Young woman, Australia[51]

- 'To feel that we are not alone is important, that there are other women doing the same work as us. To share spaces together and devise actions together gives us the strength to continue.'

Young woman leader in Nicaragua[52]

The word 'solidarity' may have gone out of fashion, but it is what women all over the world are doing under the banner of feminism to try to make the world a more equal place. We have different experiences as women and girls according to our location, class, age, ethnicity, sexuality and physical and mental abilities, and we need to recognize this as well, and to celebrate this diversity.

The hope of Phumzile Mlambo-Ngcuka, the Executive Director of UN Women, is that 'everyone will be inspired to be part of a re-energized and growing movement for gender equality. With determined people from all walks of life, and with more determined leaders, gender equality can be a defining achievement of the first quarter of the 21st century.'[53]

British feminist Rachel Holmes, who co-edited *Fifty Shades of Feminism*, writes of feminists:

'We don't have to like each other, or even wholly understand each other. We have to understand enough to work together despite our differences. Men worked that out centuries ago, and they're still doing it; men created themselves as a strategic, transnational class. Patriarchy is the most successful global movement, based on a coalition of many differences, in world history... They bury their differences for as long as and in all the ways that enable them to maintain economic, cultural and social pre-eminence. Feminism needs a new international, and a newly defined, program and strategy. You want to help organize?'[54]

Feminism is the biggest international movement the world has ever seen. So let's get out there, celebrate our differences, make a little trouble, and build a better world for us all.

1 Identities Mic, nin.tl/obamafeminist **2** *Behind the Screen,* Plan Asia, 2008. **3** Ibid. **4** Jean Casey, Charlotte Nussey and Feyi Rodway, 'Exploring the Gap: New Ideas and Old Realities: Real Choices, Real Lives: Research with young people in Brazil, Uganda and Vietnam.' Plan International, 2014. **5** Christophe Z Guilmoto, 'Sex Imbalances at Birth: Current trends, consequences and policy implications', UNFPA Asia and Pacific Regional Office, 2012; A Sen, 'Missing Women', *British Medical Journal* 1992;304(March). **6** Action Aid, nin.tl/disappearing-daughters **7** Action Aid, op cit. **8** J Evans, 'Both Halves of the Sky, nin.tl/both-halves **9** Lise Eliot, *Pink Brain, Blue Brain: How Small Differences Grow into Troublesome Gaps – and What We can Do About it,* Mariner Books, New York, 2010. **10** The Girl Child: Beijing at 10: putting policy into practice, INSTRAW, 2004. **11** Girls' Sttitudes Survey 2015, Girlguiding. nin.tl/GG-attitudes **12** Lise Eliot, op cit. **13** *Masculinities: Male Roles and Male Involvement in the Promotion of Gender Equality: Resource Packet*, Women's Commission for Refugee Women and Children, 2005. **14** Nikki van der Gaag et al, *State of the World's Girls 2011: so what about boys?*, Plan International, 2011. **15** 'On Norms and Agency Conversations about Gender Equality with Women and Men in 20 Countries', World Bank, 2012. **16** Niobe Way, *Deep Secrets: Boys' friendships and the crisis of connection*, Harvard University Press, 2011. **17** 'Tough Guise', abridged version of 'Violence, media and the crisis in masculinity', Media Education Foundation, 1999. **18** Joseph H Pleck, Freya L Sonenstein, Leighton C Ku, 'Masculinity Ideology: Its Impact on Adolescent Males' Heterosexual Relationships', *Journal of Social Issues* 1993. **19** Kirrily Pells, 'Young Lives Findings on Gender' unpublished background paper written for Plan International. younglives.org.uk **20** Nikki van der Gaag et al, *The State of the World's Girls 2014: Pathways to Power*, Plan International. **21** BBC, nin.tl/freedom-girls **22** Research conducted for *The State of the World's Girls 2011: So, What About Boys?*

Plan International. **23** In 2007, the toy industry in the US was valued at $3.2 billion according to the Department of Commerce Industry report, 'Dolls, Toys, Games, and Children's Vehicles', 2008. **24** pinkstinks.co.uk **25** *Susanna Rustin,* 'Why girls aren't pretty in pink'. *The Guardian*, 21 April 2012. **26** *John Plummer, PinkStinks: How we took on Sainsbury's – and won. Third Sector,* Haymarket, London, 2010. **27** pinkstinks.de **28** lettoysbetoys. org.uk **29** Let Toys Be Toys, nin.tl/silliness-awards **30** 'Who gets to play? What do toy ads on UK TV tell children about boys' and girls' play?, Let Toys Be Toys, 2015. **31** *The Guardian*, nin.tl/power-of-pink **32** Let Toys Be Toys, nin.tl/taking-aim **33** Pink Stinks, nin.tl/mediaps **34** Girls' Attitudes Survey 2015, op cit. **35** WHO, nin.tl/WHO-growingup **36** WHO, nin.tl/mental-health-WHO **37** Pacific Standard, nin.tl/why-men-kill-themselves **38** WHO, nin.tl/mental-health-WHO **39** Ibid **40** Feminist Campus, nin.tl/four-reasons-why **41** tostan.org/female-genital-cutting **42** Feminist Majority Foundation, nin.tl/global-fgm **43** Centre for Reproductive Rights, nin.tl/FGM-prohibitions and, more recently, BBC, nin.tl/child-marriage-outlawed **44** Spiked, nin.tl/FGM-crusade **45** tostan.org/female-genital-cutting **46** Forward UK, nin.tl/ch-marriage **47** 'Child Marriage and Female Circumcision: Evidence from Ethiopia', Young Lives Policy Brief 2014. **48** Interview by Nikki van der Gaag for the *The State of the World's Girls' Report 2014*, Plan International. **49** The Girl Effect/Nike, nin.tl/grassroots-girls **50** Interview by Nikki van der Gaag for *The State of the World's Girls 2010: Digital and Urban Frontiers*, Plan International. **51** Nick Wyatt and Simone Sandoval, 'Because I Am a Girl Research', Plan International and the Leading Edge, 2014. **52** Jean Casey, 'The Lived Reality of Young Organised Central American women: Experiences of Leadership, Empowerment and Access and Control of Economic Resources.' Unpublished research for Puntos de Encuentro, Nicaragua, 2009. **53** Progress of Women 2015, UN Women. **54** Guernica, nin.tl/50-shades-fem

Index Page numbers in **bold** refer to main subjects of boxed text.

Feminism